6.98

Corner House Publishers

SOCIAL SCIENCE REPRINTS

General Editor
MAURICE FILLER

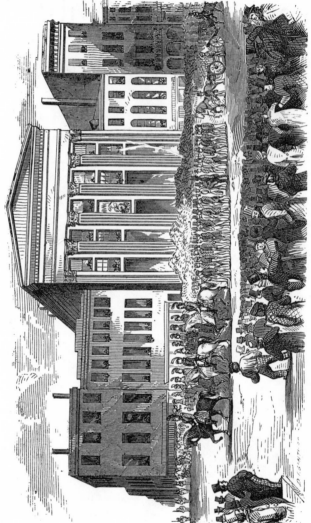

MARSHAL'S POSSE WITH BURNS MOVING DOWN STATE STREET.

ANTHONY BURNS

A HISTORY

BY

CHARLES EMERY STEVENS

CORNER HOUSE PUBLISHERS

WILLIAMSTOWN, MASSACHUSETTS 01267

1973

REPRINTED 1973

BY

CORNER HOUSE PUBLISHERS

Printed in the United States of America

" THE GEN^{R}ALL CO^{R}TE, CONCEIVING THEMSELUES BOUND BY Y^E FIRST OPORTUNITY TO BEAR WITNES AGAINST Y^E HAYNOS & CRYING SINN OF MAN STEAL- ING, AS ALSO TO P^{R}SCRIBE SUCH TIMELY REDRESSE FOR WHAT IS PAST, & SUCH A LAW FOR Y^E FUTURE AS MAY SUFFICIENTLY DETERR ALL OTH^{R}S BELONG- ING TO US TO HAVE TO DO IN SUCH VILE & MOST ODIOUS COURSES, IUSTLY ABHORED OF ALL GOOD & IUST MEN, DO ORDER, Y^T Y^E NEGRO INTERPRETER, WTH OTH^{RS} UNLAWFULLY TAKEN, BE, BY Y^E FIRST OPORTUNITY, (AT Y^E CHARGE OF Y^E COUNTRY FOR P^{R}SENT,) SENT· TO HIS NATIVE COUNTRY OF GINNY, & A LETTER WTH HIM OF Y^E INDIGNATION OF Y^E CO^{R}TE THEREABOUTS, & IUSTICE HEREOF, DESIRE- ING O^R HONO^{R}ED GOV^{R}N^R WOULD PLEASE TO PUT THIS ORDER IN EXECUTION."

Records of Massachusetts, November, 1646.

JOHN WINTHROP, *Governor.*

"Est quidem vera lex, recta ratio, naturæ congruens, diffusa in omnes, constans, sempiterna, quæ vocet ad officium jubendo, vetando a fraude deterreat, quæ tamen neque probos frustra jubet aut vetat, nec improbos jubendo aut vetando movet. Huic legi nec obrogari fas est, neque derogari ex hâc aliquid licet, neque tota abrogari potest. NEC VERO AUT PER SENATUM AUT PER POPULUM SOLVI HAC LEGE POSSUMUS, neque est quærendus explanator aut interpres ejus alius. Nec erit alia lex Romæ, alia Athenis, alia nunc, alia posthac; sed et omnes gentes, et omni tempore, una lex et sempiterna et immortalis continebit; unusque erit communis quasi magister et imperator omnium, Deus ille, legis hujus inventor, disceptator, lator; cui qui non parebit, ipse se fugiet, ac naturam hominis aspernabitur, atque hoc ipso luet maximas pœnas, etiamsi cætera supplicia quæ putantur, fugiet."

CICERO *De Republica.*

PREFACE.

THE extradition of Anthony Burns as a fugitive slave was the most memorable case of the kind that has occurred since the adoption of the Federal Constitution. It was memorable for the place and for the time of its occurrence; the place being the ancient and chief seat of Liberty in America, and the time being just the moment when the cause of Liberty had received a most wicked and crushing blow from the hand of the Federal Government. It was memorable also for the difficulty with which it was accomplished, for the intense popular excitement which it caused, for the unexampled expense which it entailed, for the grave questions of law which it involved, for the punishment which it brought down upon the head of the chief actor, and for the political revolution which it drew on. Viewing it thus, it seemed to me to merit an elaborate record; and as unusual facilities were furnished me, I ventured upon the task.

My materials have been derived chiefly from original sources. Of much that is narrated, I was myself an eye-witness. I was present at the Faneuil Hall meeting from its commencement to its close, and I witnessed the attack

1* (v)

on the Court House. Throughout the trial of Burns, save
a short interval, I had a seat within the bar, and carefully
observed the arrangements made by the Marshal, and the
demeanor of the various parties. While the troops were
drawn up on the Common, on the second of June, I passed
up and down the lines, and took note of their conduct.
Afterward, on the same day, I traversed that section
of the city from which the citizens were excluded by
force of martial law, and noticed the manner in which
the troops and the police were disposed for the purpose of
guarding the streets and avenues. Finally, I stood upon
the steps of the Custom House, when the Marshal with his
posse and prisoner passed on his way to the wharf, and
witnessed the assault of the soldiers, with sabres and bayonets, on the defenceless and unoffending multitude.

The account of the early life of Burns, of his arrest, of
his voyage back to Virginia, of his imprisonment, and of
his sojourn in North Carolina, was taken down by me from
his own lips, soon after his return to Boston. For placing
full confidence in his statements, the reader has the warrant of his former master, Col. Suttle, who, after his return to Alexandria, bore testimony to the truthfulness and
honesty of Burns in a letter which is now first printed in
this volume. I may add that he has no less warrant from
all who have known Burns.

The true history of the transactions respecting the Writ
of Replevin is here for the first time made public. It is
drawn chiefly from a correspondence (still in manuscript)

which passed between Governor Washburn and the Hon. Samuel E. Sewall, shortly after the rendition of Burns. For the use of this correspondence I am indebted to the courtesy of Governor Washburn. Some additional facts have been derived from the officer who was charged with the service of the writ.

The Rev. L. A. Grimes bore a large share in the transactions here narrated, and I have relied chiefly upon his authority in recounting such matters as came within his personal cognizance. This remark is likewise applicable to Mr. Joseph K. Hayes, who was a captain of the Boston police until the second of June, and acted a conspicuous part on that day. My acknowledgments are also due to Richard H. Dana, Jr., Esq., and Charles M. Ellis, Esq., for important documents, and for information besides.

The account of the evidence and the arguments on the examination, is abridged from the reports published at the time. The chapter relating to the trial of the Commissioner is based on facts of public notoriety, on documents published by authority of the General Court of Massachusetts, and on the original records of that body deposited in the State House.

The Appendix contains various authentic documents which are authority for certain statements in the narrative, and are otherwise illustrative of the subject. Among them are copies of letters written by District Attorney Hallett and Marshal Freeman, and on file in the office of the clerk of the Courts, at Dedham.

The Illustrations are from drawings made on the spot, by an artist who was an eye-witness of the principal scene. Adequately to depict that scene — presenting to view, as it did, tens of thousands of spectators — was impossible on a page of this size; but the picture here given will greatly assist the reader in forming a distinct conception of it. The edifices introduced into the sketches will be readily identified.

At the beginning of the volume will be found a transcript from the ancient Records of Massachusetts. The contrast between the transaction therein recorded and that presented in this narrative, will suggest its own impressive lesson. Immediately following, is a declaration of the *Higher Law* in the incomparable sentences of the great Roman Orator and Moral Philosopher.

———

As I write these lines, the country is passing through its greatest crisis of peril. On the western frontier, civil war is flagrant. At Washington, a Senator lies wounded and disabled, having been stealthily stricken down on the floor of the Senate, for words spoken in debate, by a member of the House from South Carolina. The whole South, with trifling exceptions, applauds this assault upon the representative of a sovereign State. A National Convention of the party in power has just given its sanction to the policy of which these events, as well as the extradition of Burns, are the legitimate fruits, and has nominated for the Presidency a person who has pledged himself fully to enforce that policy. Should that person be elected, and that policy be enforced, the cause of Freedom, whether in Kansas, in Washington, or in Massachusetts, would have just reason to apprehend a repetition of similar assaults from the slave power. To avert such a calamity every good citizen must labor; and I hope that this History, conceived and executed for a more general purpose, may contribute somewhat also to that particular end.

Boston, July, 1856.

CONTENTS.

(xi)

2

APPENDIX J.

APPENDIX K.

APPENDIX L.

APPENDIX M.

ANTHONY BURNS.

CHAPTER I.

IN the evening of the twenty-fourth of May, 1854, Anthony Burns was arrested as a fugitive slave in the heart of Boston. He had been employed, during the day, in a clothing store situated in Brattle street, and belonging to Coffin Pitts, a respectable colored trader. The locality was peculiarly suggestive of liberty and human rights. In full view, at the distance of only three or four rods, stands Brattle street Church, imbedded in the front face of which is a cannon-ball, preserved as a sacred memento of the Siege of Boston. A little farther off, but also in full view, stands Faneuil Hall. The street itself, an ancient one, perpetuates the name of one of the most enlightened friends of liberty that in the early days assisted in building up the Commonwealth of Massachusetts. In this favored locality Burns had passed exactly one month of quiet freedom, spent in honest industry, when the sudden interruption of his happiness took place.

The arrest was made under a warrant issued on the same day, by Edward G. Loring, a United States Commissioner.[1] The person charged with its immediate execution was a man who had already become infamous by making the hunting of fugitive slaves his special vocation. The name of this man was Asa O. Butman. He had been observed in the store of Mr. Pitts during the day; but, although he was seen more than once to fix his eye upon Burns, no suspicion had been excited by his appearance. Not dreaming of danger, Burns kept about his business until the hour of closing the shop arrived, when he locked the door and departed. It had been his constant custom to accompany his employer, with whom he boarded, directly home; but on the evening in question he took it into his head, from mere caprice, to stroll down the street in an opposite direction. Mr. Pitts meanwhile pursued his way homeward. After going on aimlessly for a few rods, Burns retraced his steps, intending to overtake his employer, who, at that moment, was disappearing round the corner of Brattle and Court streets. Apprehending nothing, he went leisurely along until, just as he had reached the corner of Hanover and Court streets, a hand was roughly laid on his shoulder, and an exclamation of, " Stop, old boy!" arrested his steps. On turning, he found himself in the grasp of Butman. Still unsuspicious of the real state of the case, and supposing that he had

[1] See Appendix A.

been beset only by a street brawler, he demanded to know why he was detained. Butman informed him that he was arrested on a charge of having broken into and robbed a jewelry-store. Conscious of innocence, and feeling assured that he could easily clear himself of the charge, Burns made no resistance, and did not even alarm his employer, who was then only two or three rods in advance. The spot where the arrest was made, was hard by Peter B. Brigham's drinking-saloon, the most noted establishment of the kind in Boston. From that, or from some other lurking-place in the vicinity, six or seven men immediately rushed forth to the assistance of the officer. Encircling the prisoner, they in a moment had him off his feet, took him in their arms horizontally as they would a dead person, and, avoiding the side-walk, rapidly bore him down the middle of the street to the Court House. At the entrance, they were received by the United States Marshal, who stood with a drawn sword upon the outer steps, manifestly awaiting their appearance. Without pause, or being set down upon his feet, the prisoner was hurried up several flights of stairs to the United States jury-room, near the top of the building. He had been informed, on being arrested, that he was to be conducted into the presence of the person whom he was accused of robbing. Finding no such person present, he now demanded to know why the jeweller did not come. Butman and his

2*

associates professed wonder at his non-appearance.
The delay continued. Suddenly, the truth flashed
upon the unhappy prisoner — he was an arrested
fugitive slave! Then, with the quickness of
thought, the whole dismal future opened up before
his mental vision. As in a dissolving view, the
land of freedom faded out, and the dark land of
slavery usurped its place. He saw himself again a
slave ; far worse than that, a slave disgraced;
pointed at as a runaway; punished; perhaps punished unto death. Overpowered by the prospect, he,
in his own simple but expressive phrase, " gave all
up." Fast confined within granite walls, and
closely guarded by eight armed men, he saw the
full hopelessness of his situation, and did not for a
moment indulge any thought of escape.

Twenty minutes had elapsed, when the door
was thrown open, and the Marshal, accompanied
by two men, entered the room. The men were
Charles F. Suttle, the claimant of Burns, and his
agent, William Brent; Virginians both. Immediately stepping toward the prisoner, Mr. Suttle,
with mock politeness, took off his hat, saluted the
latter with a low bow, and said, with emphasis on
the appellation:

" How do you do, *Mr.* Burns ? "

The prisoner had no reply for this unseemly triumph over his blasted hopes.

" Why did you run away from me?" pursued
Suttle.

"I fell asleep on board the vessel where I worked, and, before I woke up, she set sail and carried me off."

"Have n't I always treated you well, Tony?"

To this question Burns made no answer.

"Have n't I always given you money when you needed?"

"You have always given me twelve and a half-cents once a year."

Nothing further passed between the two, but in this brief colloquy Burns had already made admissions decisive of his fate. While it was going on, Brent stood gazing steadily in the prisoner's face, but exchanged no words, not even salutations with him. The object of the wily slaveholder had been accomplished, and with his friend he now took his departure. As he passed out, the Marshal put the inquiry, "Well, that's the man, is it?" to which Suttle responded, "Yes."

No sooner had they gone, than the door was again strongly barred, and Burns was left to pass the night with the men by whom he had been arrested. Recalling his thoughts from Suttle, he now turned with indignant scorn upon Butman.

"I thought," said he, "you arrested me for *stealing*."

"I was afraid of a mob," replied the dastard, "and that was the reason why I did n't arrest you when you left the store." He added that he had been standing on the opposite side of the street, watching for Burns.

" If you had told me the truth, it would n't have been so easy a job to arrest me," said the stalwart slave.[1]

" If you had resisted, I should have shot you down," was the retort of the slave-hunter.

Butman rightly judged that a lie was necessary to the success of his enterprise. Had Burns suspected the truth, he might have been slain, but he would never have been captured. His flashing eye and deepened tones, as well as his words, gave assurance of this, as he spoke of the subject afterward.

Butman and his fellow catchpolls had no thought of putting themselves to any personal discomfort. Belonging to a class of men who are governed by their sensual appetites, they reckoned upon riotous living at the expense of the Government as a part of their reward. So infamous was the business put upon them, and so few were the persons who would undertake it, that they in a measure had the Government in their power, and could make their own terms. Accordingly, no sooner were they well housed for the night, with their prisoner, than various choice viands, which had been ordered by them from a neighboring refectory, were introduced into the apartment. With these unwonted luxuries they at once proceeded to gorge themselves, while Burns, who had tasted no food since noon, was left to pass the night fasting.

[1] Burns was about six feet in height, broad chested, and otherwise firmly built.

Having finished their repast, they beguiled the hours with card-playing. Tiring of this, they next fell to entertaining Burns with talk about Sims, of whom, once a prisoner in the same room like himself, he now heard for the first time. At last, having exhausted their resources, they stretched themselves out in various postures, and one after another sunk into sleep. As may well be imagined, there was no sleep that night for Burns; seated in his chair, statue-like, the hours flew by him unheeded, while his great calamity stood ever present staring him in the face.

With the next dawn, his keepers awoke to indulge their appetites afresh, a liberal supply of intoxicating liquors being, as before, an important item in their bill of fare. Burns was now for the first time invited to join them in their refreshments, but he loathed food and declined the invitation. His coarse and sensual jailers, unable to comprehend what nature should have taught them, imputed his refusal to obstinacy, and muttered that " it was not worth while for him to make a d—d fool of himself."

In a short time, Riley, the deputy marshal, entered the room and ordered handcuffs to be brought; they were procured by the ever ready Butman. With these Burns was manacled, and in that condition was forthwith conducted to the United States court-room on the floor below. Suttle and Brent were already there; the Marshal and ten or twelve persons in his interest were the only

others in the room. Burns was placed in the prisoner's seat, opposite the judges' bench, where he
remained handcuffed, with Butman and one of his
aids, armed with revolvers, seated on each side
of him. In a few minutes after, Commissioner
Loring entered the room, and the proceedings in
the case forthwith commenced.

As yet, the public had received no hint of the
arrest; the morning papers of the city were dumb;
apparently, the affair had escaped the vigilance of
the ubiquitous reporters. It was the purpose and
hope of all the parties concerned to hasten the examination, and, if possible, remove the prisoner
beyond reach before any rumor of their proceedings
should get abroad. Unfortunately for the success
of their design, Richard H. Dana, Jr., happened to
pass the Court House just before nine o'clock, the
hour set for the examination, and received an in-
timation of what was going on within. He immediately turned his steps and entered the court-
room. Making his way through some opposition
to the side of Burns, he offered the latter his professional services. The prisoner declined them.
"It will be of no use," he said; "they have got me."
He added, that, if he protracted the matter by
making a defence, it would be worse for him after
getting back to Virginia. The humane lawyer
reasoned the matter with him; the case, he said,
depended on certain papers and records in which
some flaw might be detected. Even the men who
guarded him, betrayed, for the moment, into a better

impulse by his aspect of despair, joined in urging
him to make a defence.[1] Others, also, including
Charles M. Ellis and Theodore Parker, who had
before this time entered the room, attempted, but
without success, to persuade him to make a stand.

The Commissioner making his appearance at
this juncture as before stated, Mr. Dana at once
went up and spoke to him privately. Burns, he
said, was paralyzed with fear, and in a condition
wholly unfit to act for himself. He suggested that
the Commissioner should endeavor to ascertain the
real wishes of Burns in the matter; and that for
this purpose he should call the prisoner to the
bench, instead of addressing him while in the dock,
with Suttle sitting between them, as he was, and
gazing into the prisoner's face. " I intend to do
so," replied the Commissioner.

The examination now proceeded. The counsel
for the claimant read the warrant for the arrest,
with the officer's return upon it, and presented the
record from the Virginia court required by the
fugitive slave act. Brent was then put upon the

[1] See Mr. Dana's testimony before the committee of the legislature on the subject of removing Mr. Loring from the office of
Judge of Probate. He adds : " I have heard that Burns said that
afterward some of the officers advised him differently, and tried to
make him suspect us." Mr. Parker's testimony on this point before
the same committee was this : " One of the ruffians that guarded
him said, ' You may ask him as many times as you have a mind to ;
you will never get him to have counsel or make any defence.' The
other man who guarded him on the other side said, ' Well, Mr.
Parker, it will do no harm to try, and I hope he will.' "

stand as a witness to prove the identity of the prisoner with the person named in the warrant. His testimony was received without interruption, until he was asked to state the admissions made by Burns to Suttle while in custody the night before. At this point Mr. Dana interposed. He had remained quiet thus far, supposing that, after the claimant had made out his case, the Commissioner intended to redeem his pledge by calling Burns to the bench and ascertaining if he desired to make a defence. But he now saw that the prisoner should at once have counsel to object to the introduction of improper testimony. Accordingly he rose, and, addressing the court as *amicus curiæ*, urged the propriety of delay. The motion was resisted by the claimant's counsel. Burns, it was said, had admitted that he was Suttle's slave, and did not desire a defence; and it was broadly hinted that the only object of those who sought delay was for public purposes of their own. Disdaining to reply to this charge, Mr. Dana continued to press his point with great earnestness. He was followed by Mr. Ellis, who also addressed the court as *amicus curiæ*.

At the conclusion of these addresses, the Commissioner directed the officer to bring Burns to him. This was done, after the manacles were covertly removed from his hands. The Commissioner then addressed him in a kind manner, told him what the claim was, inquired if he wished to make a defence, and informed him that he could have counsel if he desired. Burns looked round the court-room timidly, and made no reply.

"Anthony," said the Commissioner, "would you like to go away and come back here and meet me to-morrow or next day, and tell me what you want to do?"

Mr. Dana watched him closely, but could not see whether he indicated assent or dissent. The Commissioner was also in doubt, but after a moment said,

"Anthony, I understand you to say you would?"

"I should," at length replied Burns.

"Then it shall be so," said the Commissioner, and the prisoner was conducted back to his seat.

The presence of Theodore Parker has been mentioned. He afterward described his interview with Burns, and the appearance of the latter, in the presence of Suttle. "As no counsel had been assigned," said he, "I conferred with Burns. I told him I was a minister, and had been appointed at a meeting of citizens, minister at large in behalf of fugitive slaves, and asked him if he did not want counsel. He said, 'I shall have to go back. Mr. Suttle knows me — Brent knows me. If I must go back, I want to go back as easy as I can.' 'But surely,' I said, 'it can do you no harm to make a defence.' 'Well,' said Burns, 'you may do as you have a mind to about it.' He seemed to me to be stupefied with fear; and when he talked with me, he kept looking at Suttle and Brent. His eye wandered from me, as an insane man's eye wanders, and fixed itself on Suttle. When Loring asked him whether he would have counsel, his eye fluctuated from Loring to Suttle, and back again to Loring, and when he said, ' Yes,' he turned away from Suttle to do so."

The examination was adjourned until Saturday, the twenty-seventh day of the month; and when the court re-opened on that morning, a further adjournment till the Monday following was ordered, on the ground of the lateness of the hour when the prisoner's counsel had been appointed. Meanwhile, Burns was again manacled and taken back to the jury-room, where he remained, under the constant surveillance of four armed keepers, from Thursday until Monday. The interval was industriously employed by these tools of the slaveholder in the livery of the Federal Government, in attempts to lead Burns into making admissions fatal to himself. All the cunning of their base natures was called into play to compass their end. They made the warmest professions of friendship for him, and invoked the direst curses on their souls if they did not make their professions good. They plied him with questions which, quietly assuming the fact that he was Suttle's slave, looked toward information on unimportant points. Thus they inquired whether Suttle "raised or bought him." In this instance Burns proved too shrewd for them, and told them to find out some other way.

Still pursuing their object, they sought to get him committed in writing. On entering the jury-room on Friday, Mr. Grimes, a clergyman of Boston, found Burns in the act of dictating a letter to Suttle, and one of his keepers acting as an amanuensis. Burns had been persuaded to take this step by the artful suggestions of the official. The people of Boston, this fellow said, were laboring under the impression that Suttle had been a hard master to Burns; this tended to irritate Suttle; but if Burns would dictate a statement to the contrary, it would cause his master to feel more kindly toward him. Ascertaining these facts, Mr. Grimes administered so stern a rebuke to the fellow that he stammered out an apology, and promised to destroy the letter. Nothing, however, was farther from his thoughts; and Burns, now made aware that the letter was to be used as an instrument against him, sought to get it into his possession. After some delay, it was delivered into his hands for the purpose of making some addition to it, and by him was immediately destroyed.

Following their natural bent, these servants of the Federal Government invited their prisoner to join them in gambling for money. His reply was, that he never played cards. They professed to think it strange that he should refuse; Sims, they said, had played with them and won a number of dollars. They next urged him to entertain them with negro melodies, and again cited the example of Sims in support of their request. But Burns replied, with a pathos that was wasted upon their hard natures, — " My singing days are over. I have now learned another song." Beginning at length to suspect the religious character of their prisoner, one of them jeeringly requested Burns to pray for him. " I trust I shall do that," was the simple reply.

Thus did Burns pass the hours of his imprisonment, alternately the object of treacherous interrogations and the sport of scoffers. Thus did officers of the Federal Government, not content with the infamy attaching even to the strict and decorous discharge of their function, add thereto the ineffable meanness of seeking to inveigle their prisoner into some unguarded act or expression, with which they might hasten to the slaveholder, and claim a reward.

CHAPTER II.

THE news of Burns's arrest quickly spread through the city. It found the public mind in a very different frame from what it had been in at the arrest of Sims, three years before. Those who had been most zealous, on that occasion, for the execution of the fugitive slave act, now stood passive, or openly expressed their indignation at this new attempt. No immediate step was taken, however, except by an association styled a Committee of Vigilance. This association took its origin from the passage of the fugitive slave act. Its sole object was to defeat, in all cases, the execution of that hated statute. Thoroughly organized under a written code of laws, with the necessary officers and working committees arranged on the principle of a subdivision of labor, with wealth and professional talent at its command, actuated by the most determined purpose and operating in secret, it was well fitted to strike powerful blows for the accomplishment of its object. The roll of its members displayed the most diversified assemblage of characters, but this diversity only secured its greater efficiency. The white and the colored

3*   (29)

race, freeborn sons of Massachusetts and fugitive
slaves from the South, here co-operated together.
Among them were men of fine culture, and of
high social position; men too of renown. Some
of the rich men of Boston were enrolled in this
committee. A most important portion consisted
of members of the Suffolk Bar, by whose counsels
the committee were guided through the legal
perils of their undertaking. The treasury was
bountifully supplied by voluntary contributions.
One gave of his poverty what he could, while
another subscribed his five hundred dollars. The
methods of operation were various. Whatever
tended to keep the victim from falling into the
grasp of the law, or to rescue him if haply he had
already fallen in, was legitimate to their purpose.
If a fugitive slave arrived in Boston, he was at
once taken in charge. In case there was no pursuit, he remained at ease; but otherwise, he was
dispatched at the expense of the Committee on his
way to Canada. Sometimes the officers of the
law were notified that a certain vessel with a fugitive slave on board would arrive at the port of
Boston on a day named; but this Committee of
Vigilance had also been notified, and, while the
officers were waiting on the wharf for the vessel to
come up, the agents of the Committee had taken
boat, boarded the ship far out in the harbor, withdrawn the slave, — perhaps under a show of legal
authority, — and landed him at some solitary point
on shore, where a carriage was in waiting by which

he was placed beyond the reach of pursuit.
Whenever a slaveholder arrived in the city, he
was watched and the object of his visit inquired
into. If he had come in the pursuit of ordinary
business, he was left alone, but the slightest indi-
cation that he was in pursuit of a slave, sufficed to
place him under a surveillance that never ceased
while he remained in the city. On one occasion,
a female slave, while walking in the streets of
Boston, suddenly beheld her owner a short distance off, approaching toward her. She turned
and fled down another street, notified some of the
Committee of the apparition, and the same night
was removed from the city. The slaveholder was
traced to his hotel, and never lost sight of afterwards. Night and day, his steps were dogged by
members of the Committee. When one had followed him a certain length of time, he was passed
over to another; now it was a white man, and
now a colored man, that, like his shadow, pursued
him wherever he went. It was afterward ascertained that he had come to Boston in pursuit of
the very slave by whom he had been recognized,
but who had fortunately escaped recognition by
him.

By this Committee of Vigilance, the case of
Burns was now taken in hand. Early in the afternoon of the day following his arrest, a full meeting for the purpose was secretly convened. On
the main point there was but one voice; all agreed
that, be the Commissioner's decision what 't might,

Burns should never be taken back to Virginia, if it were in their power to prevent. But there were two opinions as to the method by which they should proceed to effect their purpose. One party counselled an attack on the Court House, and a forcible rescue of the prisoner. The other party were in favor of a less violent course. They proposed to await the Commissioner's decision; then, if it were adverse to the prisoner, they would crowd the streets when he was brought forth, present an impassable living barrier to the progress of the escort, and see to it that, in the *melee* which would inevitably follow, Burns made good his escape. Both plans were long and vehemently debated, but, without arriving at any decision, the meeting was adjourned till evening. At this second session, the more peaceful method prevailed by a very large majority. For the purpose of arousing the popular feeling to the requisite pitch and also indicating to the public the particular line of action which had been chosen, it was at the same time decided to call a public meeting in Faneuil Hall for the evening following. Another step was, to detail a certain number of men to watch the Court House, night and day, lest the prisoner should be removed unawares. Some, in the excess of their apprehensions, feared that the Commissioner might hold a midnight session of his court, and send Burns back into slavery under cover of darkness. For the convenience of this watch, a wealthy member of the association threw open the loft of his warehouse and liberally furnished it with provisions.

The advocates for an assault on the Court House, though outvoted, were not to be beaten off from their purpose. At the close of the evening meeting, a voice loudly called upon all who were in favor of that mode of action, to tarry after the rest had retired. Fifteen or twenty persons responded to this call; but when it was proposed that they should pledge themselves in writing to engage with force and arms in the perilous enterprise, only seven of the number had the courage to affix their signatures to the agreement. Not dismayed by such severe sifting, these seven still resolved to go forward; and the following night — the night for the meeting in Faneuil Hall — was fixed upon for the execution of their plan.

On Friday morning, the call for that meeting appeared in all the papers and was placarded throughout the city. " To secure justice for a man claimed as a slave by a Virginia kidnapper, and imprisoned in Boston Court House, in defiance of the laws of Massachusetts " — thus began the notice. " Shall he be plunged into the hell of Virginia slavery by a Massachusetts Judge of Probate ? " — was the more ominous interrogatory with which it closed. By eight o'clock in the evening, the venerable Hall was filled to overflowing. The assembly was called to order by Samuel E. Sewall, a distinguished citizen of Boston. George R. Russell, an ex-mayor of the neighboring city of

Roxbury, was placed in the President's chair, while among the Vice-Presidents were several gentlemen who had been of the Governor's Council, together with Dr. Samuel G. Howe, the distinguished philanthropist and historian of the Greek Revolution. Dr. Henry I. Bowditch and Robert Morris, the colored lawyer of Boston, filled the post of Secretaries.

The subject of the evening was introduced by the President in language of sarcasm and irony. " I once thought," said he, " that a fugitive could never be taken from Boston. I was mistaken! One has been taken from among us, and another lies in peril of his liberty. The boast of the slaveholder is, that he will catch his slaves under the shadow of Bunker Hill. We have made compromises until we find that compromise is concession, and concession is degradation. The question has come at last, whether the North will still consent to do what it is held base to do at the south. When Henry Clay was asked whether it was expected that northern men would catch slaves for the slaveholders, he replied: ' No! of course not! We will never expect you to do what we hold it *base* to do.' Now, the very men who had acquiesced with Mr. Clay, demand of us that we catch their slaves. It seems that the Constitution has nothing for us to do but to help catch fugitive slaves! When we get Cuba and Mexico as slave states, when the foreign slave trade is re-established with all the appalling horrors of the Middle Passage,

and the Atlantic is again filled with the bodies of
dead Africans, then we may think it time to
awaken to our duty. God grant that we may do
so soon! The time will come when slavery will
pass away, and our children shall have only its
hideous memory to make them wonder at the
deeds of their fathers. For one, I hope to *die* in a
land of liberty — in a land which no slave-hunter
shall dare pollute with his presence."

Dr. Howe presented a series of resolves that
were subsequently adopted by the assembly as the
expression of its sentiments. They embodied these
epigrammatic sentences: " The time has come to
declare and to demonstrate the fact that no slave-
hunter can carry his prey from the Commonwealth
of Massachusetts." — " That which is not just is not
law, and that which is not law ought not to be
obeyed." — " Resistance to tyrants is obedience to
God." — " Nothing so well becomes Faneuil Hall,
as the most determined resistance to a bloody and
overshadowing despotism." — " It is the will of
God that every man should be free; we will as
God wills; God's will be done." — " No man's
freedom is safe unless all men are free."

One of the ex-councillors of state gave his
voice for "fighting." John L. Swift, a young
lawyer of fervid oratory, next addressed the assembly. " Burns," said he, " is in the Court House.
Is there any law to keep him there ? If we allow
Marshal Freeman to carry away that man, then
the word, ' Cowards,' should be stamped upon our

foreheads. When we go from this Cradle of
Liberty, let us go to the tomb of liberty, the Court
House. To-morrow, Burns will have remained incarcerated there three days, and I hope to-morrow
to witness, in his release, the resurrection of
liberty."

There were two men in the Hall for whose
words, more than for those of all others, the assembly impatiently waited. These were Wendell
Phillips and Theodore Parker. Regarded by the
public as the leaders of the present enterprise,
closely associated in spirit and purpose, and
eminent, both, for the power of speech, they yet differed from each other in many particulars. Mr.
Phillips belonged to the aristocracy, so far as such
a class may be supposed to exist in this country.
He had an ancestry to boast of; his family name
was interwoven with the history of the Commonwealth; and some of those who had borne it had
filled high offices in the government. Mr. Parker,
on the other hand, was of more plebeian origin; he
had been the architect of his own fortunes, and
was by far the most distinguished person of his
lineage. In religion, Mr. Phillips was a Calvinist,
and believed that the Holy Scriptures were the inspired word of God; while Mr. Parker, rejecting
all creeds and disowned by all sects, held the Bible
to contain only the wisdom of fallible men, and
claimed for himself and for future sages the possible
power of improving thereon. Mr. Phillips was a
lawyer, but he seldom appeared in the courts; Mr.

Parker was a clergyman, and, though without a church and eschewing the holy sacraments, preached constantly to a large but shifting congregation. Mr. Phillips excelled in oratory, Mr. Parker was a greater master of the pen. The former studied men, the latter, books. Mr. Parker had a wider reputation — Europe had heard of him; but those who knew both would have forsaken him to hang upon the lips of Mr. Phillips. Mr. Parker had secured his triumph when he had uttered his speech; Mr. Phillips found his chief satisfaction in the accomplishment of the end at which his oratory was aimed. Mr. Phillips had the garb and gait of a gentleman; Mr. Parker, as he moved along with stumbling steps and prone looks, had the aspect of a recluse student. In their physical characteristics, they differed not less than in mental and moral traits. Mr. Phillips was a person of commanding height and elegant proportions; his features were cast in the Roman mould, his head was rounded and balanced almost to the ideal standard. A ruddy complexion, fair hair, and eyes of sparkling blue, showed him to be of the true Saxon race. Mr. Parker, on the contrary, was of inferior stature and ungraceful form; he had the face of a Diogenes, and his massive head, capacious of brain in the frontal region, was not symmetrically developed. He had an atrabiliar complexion, dark hair, and large, dark eyes that looked forth from behind spectacles with a steady, unwinking gaze.

4

The speeches of both, on the present occasion, were so imperfectly reported that the public abroad had but a faint conception of their power and effect. Mr. Phillips was the first to speak.

" The city government is on our side," began the orator; a storm of cheers greeted the announcement. " I am glad," continued he, " to hear the applause of that sentiment. If the city police had been warned on the Sims case, as they are now, not to lift a finger in behalf of the kidnappers, under pain of instant dismissal, Thomas Sims would have been here in Boston to-day. To-morrow is to determine whether we are ready to do the duty they have left us to do. There is now no law in Massachusetts, and when law ceases, the people may act in their own sovereignty. I am against squatter sovereignty in Nebraska, and against kidnappers' sovereignty in Boston. See to it, that to-morrow, in the streets of Boston, you ratify the verdict of Faneuil Hall, that Anthony Burns has no master but his God.

" The question is to be settled to-morrow, whether we shall adhere to the case of Shadrach or the case of Sims. Will you adhere to the case of Sims, and see this man carried down State Street, between two hundred men ? I have been talking seventeen years about slavery, and it seems to me I have talked to little purpose, for within three years, two slaves can be carried away from Boston. Nebraska, I call knocking a man down, and this is spitting in his face after he is down. When

I heard of this case, and that Burns was locked up in that Court House, my heart sank within me.

"See to it, every one of you, as you love the honor of Boston, that you watch this case so closely that you can look into that man's eyes. When he comes up for trial, get a sight at him, and don't lose sight of him. There is nothing like the mute eloquence of a suffering man to urge to duty; be there, and I will trust the result. If Boston streets are to be so often desecrated by the sight of returning fugitives, let us be there, that we may tell our children we saw it done. There is now no use for Faneuil Hall. Faneuil Hall is the purlieus of the Court House to-morrow morning, where the children of Adams and Hancock may prove that they are not bastards. Let us prove that we are worthy of liberty."

Theodore Parker followed his coadjutor. Addressing the assembly as "fellow subjects of Virginia," he poured forth a torrent of the most bitter invective. At the close,[1] he proposed that when the meeting adjourned, it should be to meet in Court Square, the following morning, at nine o'clock. "To-night," shouted a hundred voices in reply. The speaker stood silent, as one in doubt. At length he called on those who were in favor of proceeding that night to the Square, to raise their hands: half the assembly did so. But now the excitement burst through all bounds,—the vast Hall was filled with one wild roar of voices. "To

[1] See Appendix M

the Court House," was shouted in one quarter; "to the Revere House for the slave-catchers," was answered back from another.   In vain Mr. Parker attempted to allay the tumult, — his voice was submerged in the billows of sound, and he stood gesticulating like one in a dumb show.   A potent master of the weapons that are fitted to goad the public mind even to madness, he lacked the sovereign power to control and subdue at will large masses of men.   Amid the uproar, Wendell Phillips again ascended the platform.   The different quality of the two men then appeared.   Ere half a dozen sentences had fallen from his lips, the assembly had subsided into profound stillness.

" Let us remember," said he, "where we are and what we are going to do.   You have said, to-night, you will vindicate the fair fame of Boston.   Let me tell you, you won't do it by groaning at the slave-catchers at the Revere House — by attempting the impossible act of insulting a slave-catcher. If there is a man here who has an arm and a heart ready to sacrifice anything for the freedom of an oppressed man, let him do it to-morrow.   If I thought it would be done to-night, I would go first. I don't profess courage, but I do profess this : when there is a possibility of saving a slave from the hands of those who are called officers of the law, I am ready to trample any statute or any man under my feet to do it, and am ready to help any one hundred men to do it.   But wait until the day-time.   The vaults of the banks in State street sym-

pathize with us. The Whigs, who have been kicked
once too often, sympathize with us. It is in your
power so to block up every avenue, that the man cannot be carried off. Do not, then, balk the effort of
to-morrow by foolish conduct to-night, giving the
enemy the alarm. You that are ready to do the real
work, be not carried away by indiscretion which
may make shipwreck of our hopes. The zeal that
won't keep till to-morrow will never free a slave."

By this time the orator had his audience well in
hand, when suddenly a man at the entrance of the
Hall shouted: "Mr. Chairman, I am just informed
that a mob of negroes is in Court Square attempting to rescue Burns. I move that we adjourn to
Court Square." A formal vote was not waited
for, and the next instant the whole mass was pouring down the broad stairs and along the streets
toward the new theatre of action.

It is necessary to return and follow the movements of the little band that had pledged themselves to the forcible rescue of Burns. A place of
rendezvous had been appointed, but when the time
for meeting arrived, only six of the seven appeared.
The defection of their faint-hearted companion did
not shake the purpose of the rest. Feeling, however, that their number was too small, they agreed
to go forth, and, if possible, secure each man six
coadjutors. This effort was so successful that
in a short time the number of confederates was
increased to nearly twenty-five. Their weapons
of attack were various; some were armed with

4*

revolvers, some carried axes, and some butcher's cleavers that had just been purchased and were left in their paper coverings for better concealment. In a passage-way hard by, a large stick of timber had been secretly deposited to serve as a battering-ram. Soon after nine o'clock, everything was ready for the assault. It was at this juncture that the alarm had been given to the meeting in Faneuil Hall.

Scarcely had the crowd from the Hall begun to pour into the Square when the assault was commenced. The lamps that lighted the Square had already been extinguished, so that under cover of darkness the assailants might more easily escape detection. Strangely neglecting the eastern entrance, which was not secured at the time,[1] they passed round to the west side and commenced the attack in that quarter. The Court House on that side presented to the eye an unbroken façade of granite two hundred feet long and four stories high. In the lower part were three entrances, closed by massive two-leaved doors which were secured by heavy locks and bolts. Against the middle one of these doors, the beam which had been previously provided, was now brought to bear with all the force that ten or twelve men could muster. At the same moment, one or two others plied their axes against the panels. As the quick, heavy

---

[1] Col. Suttle happened to be in the Court House at the time, and escaped by the east door after the attack commenced, leaving to Batchelder and others the business of defending his property at the risk and sacrifice of their lives.

NIGHT ATTACK ON THE COURT HOUSE.

blows resounded through the Square, the crowd, every moment rapidly increasing, sent up their wild shouts of encouragement, while some hurled missiles against the windows, and others discharged their pistols in the same direction. In two or three minutes, a panel in one part of the door had been beaten through; the other part had been partially forced back on its hinges, when the assailants found their entrance obstructed by defenders within. The Marshal, whose office was in the building, although not anticipating the attack, was not altogether unprepared for it. In the course of the day, he had appointed fifty special aids, and posted them in different parts of the spacious building; he had also caused to be deposited in his office a large quantity of cutlasses. On the first alarm, the specials were hastily armed with these weapons and set to defend the assaulted door. As often as the pressure from without forced it partially open, it was closed again and braced by the persons of those inside. While thus engaged, one of the Marshal's men, a truckman named Batchelder, suddenly drew back from the door, exclaiming that he was stabbed. He was carried into the Marshal's office and laid upon the floor, where he almost immediately expired. It was discovered that a wound, several inches in length, had been inflicted by some sharp instrument in the lower part of his abdomen, whereby an artery had been severed, causing him to bleed to death. A conflict of opinion afterward arose respecting the source from whence the blow proceeded. Some affirmed that it was an accident caused by one of his own party. It was said that Batchelder was engaged at the moment in bracing one part of the door with his shoulders; that while he was in that half-stooping posture, another of the specials, seeing through the opening the hands of one of the assailants, aimed at them a blow with a watchman's club, which, missing its mark, fell upon the head of Batchelder and drove him down upon the blade of his own cutlass. Another, and perhaps more probable account was, that while Batchelder stood bracing the door behind the broken panel, the wound was inflicted by an arm thrust through from the outside, not with any murderous intent, but to compel him to relax his hold.

In the temporary confusion within, caused by this fatal result, the leader of the assailants, the Rev. Thomas W. Higginson, succeeded in forcing his way into the building. None followed him, and the door was almost instantly closed again. For a moment he was alone, face to face with his adversaries; the next, he re-appeared on the outside, exclaiming to his associates, " You cowards, will you desert us now?"[1] A sabre cut across the chin, and other marks, attested the rough reception he had encountered while within the walls. The courage and daring displayed by this person showed him to be a fit leader in such an enterprise. He could trace his lineage directly back to one of

---

[1] Two others, of those engaged in the attack, effected an entrance a few moments later, and after Mr. Higginson's repulse.

the most distinguished of those who with Endicott at Salem began the foundations of the Commonwealth. Almost at the same moment with his repulse, eight or nine of his companions were seized by the police, who had quietly mingled in the crowd, and were borne off to the watch-house. Intimidated by this sudden and successful movement, and weakened by the loss of their comrades, the rest made no further attempt, and very soon the crowd began to disperse.

The room in which Burns was confined, was on the side of the building against which the attack was directed, and in one of the upper stories. Burns had received a hint of the intended assault, but his keepers were entirely unprepared for it. The first sounds made by the assailants below, filled them with extreme terror. Abandoning their customary pastime of card-playing, they hastened to extinguish the light, and to close the blinds at the windows. Burns was then placed against the wall between the two windows, for security against any chance shot that might enter the room, while they themselves crouched upon the floor in the farthest corner. A box of pistols and cutlasses had been placed in the room on the same day; this, Burns was forbidden to approach. Their position did not justify such an excess of fear. The extreme height of the room from the ground placed it beyond the reach of danger from the outside, while the door was barricaded by seven massive iron bars extending from top to bottom at intervals of not

more than a foot.[1] Had the assailants succeeded
in clearing their way through all other opposition,
this formidable barrier alone was sufficient to have
held them in check until the arrival of a military
force.

In another part of the building, the judges of the
Supreme Court of Massachusetts were assembled
at the same hour, awaiting the return of a jury.
Some of the latter having incautiously put their
heads out of the window to ascertain the nature of
the tumult, were fired at indiscriminately, to the
serious danger of their lives.

In the City Hall, hard by, the Mayor, with several
officers of the municipal government, happened to
be present at the same hour. Notified by the
Chief of Police of the state of affairs, he at once
ordered out two companies of artillery. Both arrived on the ground before midnight, and were stationed, the one in the Court House, the other in

---

[1] The room in which Burns was confined, is indicated in the preceding engraving by the lighted window in the third story. It was
a jury-room, and one of several which the County of Suffolk had
leased to the United States for the accommodation of the federal
courts. As Massachusetts had prohibited the use of her prisons
and jails for the confinement of fugitive slaves, the jury-room had
been converted into a cell for that purpose. The bars were placed
across the door on the occasion of Sims' arrest. Immediately after
the extradition of Burns, the United States received a notice to quit
the premises in thirty days, which was done, and the federal courts
were removed to a private dwelling temporarily fitted up. The
iron bars with their fastenings were removed, and the room was
afterwards partially destroyed, (perhaps purified also,) by a fire that
seriously threatened the destruction of the whole building.

the City Hall.   At the same time, the Marshal dispatched his deputy to procure a body of United States troops.   Proceeding to East Boston, the deputy there chartered a steamer, directed his course with all speed to Fort Warren, and took on board a corps of marines under command of Maj. S. C. Ridgley.   In six hours after, they were quartered within the walls of the Court House. Another company of marines was dispatched from the Navy Yard in Charlestown, on the requisition of the Marshal, and was also quartered in the same building.

CHAPTER III.

THE attempt to release Burns from duress by violence having failed, steps were taken to accomplish the same object by legal process. For this purpose resort was had to the Writ of Personal Replevin. This writ is one of those great safeguards which every free state is careful to provide for protecting the liberty of its citizens. Less famous than the Writ of Habeas Corpus, it is in some respects more valuable than that, more efficacious in securing the end for which both were instituted, and not less worthy to be maintained in full operative vigor. To obtain the writ of habeas corpus, special application must be made to a judge on the bench or in chambers, and it rests with him to grant or refuse it at his option; often it is refused. The writ of replevin, on the other hand, issues of course and of right; the prisoner, or any personal friend, or any stranger acting in his behalf, may cause it to be made at pleasure. As in the case of ordinary writs, blank forms bearing the name of the Chief Justice abound; one of these is filled up by an attorney or some competent person, and placed in the hands of an officer, upon whom,

(48)

from that moment, it becomes imperative. Under the habeas corpus writ, no trial by jury can be had; the judge alone hears the case, and sets the prisoner at liberty or remands him into custody, as he sees fit. The great benefit of the writ of replevin is, that it secures a trial by jury. The judge, under the habeas corpus, will be certain to remand the prisoner if he finds that he is legally held; he will not consider the question of the prisoner's inherent right to his liberty. But in the trial under the writ of replevin, the prisoner may demand a verdict upon the question whether he is righteously restrained of his liberty, whatever the legal aspects of the duress.[1]

This great popular writ was one of the most ancient known to the common law of England. As such, it was introduced into the English colonies in America. In Massachusetts, it remained a part of the unwritten, or common law, from the earliest period until the year 1786, when its provisions were incorporated into a statute. For a period of half a century, this statute continued unchanged and in full force; then, by the enactment of the Revised Statutes in 1836, the Writ of Personal Replevin was abolished. By positive

---

[1] In Massachusetts, every person restrained of his liberty is now entitled, *as of right and of course*, to the writ of habeas corpus. This privilege was secured by the act known as the "Personal Liberty Law," which was passed by two-thirds of both Houses over the veto of Governor Gardner, May 21, 1855. The extradition of Burns was the immediate cause of this legislation.

enactment it ceased to form a part, not only of the written, but also of the unwritten law of the Commonwealth. The watchful friends of liberty at once sounded the alarm, and in 1837 the Writ in all its pristine vigor was restored to the statute book, where it still remained at the time of Burns' arrest.

The first use of this instrument, for the relief of Burns, was made on the day following his arrest. A writ of replevin was at that time made by Seth Webb, Jr., and delivered to Coroner Charles Smith, who forthwith served it upon the United States Marshal. The answer of the latter was a quiet refusal to comply with the mandate of the writ, on the ground that he held Burns by legal process. No effort was made to enforce compliance; the writ was returned into court with the proper indorsement; and thus, for the moment, the matter rested.

On Sunday, May twenty-eighth, the subject was revived at an informal meeting of certain members of the Boston Board of Aldermen, held for the purpose at the office of the Chief of Police, who was also present. A rescue of Burns from the custody of the Marshal before the Commissioner's decision should be pronounced, they did not propose. But it was thought that after the decision, an interval of time might occur when a writ of replevin could be served without involving a conflict with the United States officers. Coroner Smith was summoned to attend the conference.

On appearing, he was asked if he would undertake to serve the writ at such a time as the one
mentioned. With some hesitation he agreed to
do so, provided the sanction of the Governor,
Attorney-General, and City Solicitor of Boston
were first obtained. This answer was thought
satisfactory and the conference ended. On the
next day, the Coroner and Alderman Dunham
sought an interview on the subject with City Solicitor Hillard. The Solicitor gave it as his opinion
that no such interval of time as they contemplated
would occur, and strongly advised them against
proceeding with the writ.

While this was passing, two citizens of Boston, Samuel E. Sewall and Henry I. Bowditch,
were moving in another direction and with a
bolder purpose. Mr. Sewall was a lineal descend-
ant of that ancient Chief Justice of Massachusetts
who, having been betrayed by the spirit of the age
into giving his judicial sanction to the prosecutions
for witchcraft, soon vindicated his innate noble-
ness by a solemn act of repentance in a public
assembly of his fellow-citizens. The finer qualities of this Puritan judge re-appeared in Mr.
Sewall. A man of pure and upright life, an
eminent lawyer, a wise and incorruptible friend of
public liberty, he naturally rose to be a conspicious
character, and was more than once honored with
the nomination and support of his party for the
office of Governor. Mr. Bowditch was the son of
America's most illustrious mathematician, the

interpreter of Laplace. He was a physician of eminence, and, like Mr. Sewall, uncompromisingly hostile to the fugitive slave act.

It was the desire of these gentlemen to have a writ of replevin served with instant dispatch; they were quite prepared to deliver Burns from duress without waiting for the Commissioner's decision. But there was a serious difficulty in the way. Burns was in the custody of an officer who had expressed a determination to resist the state process, and who had a strong civil and military force to back him. It was plain that if the writ was to be efficiently served, if Burns was to be taken out of the Marshal's hands, it could only be done by the aid of a force sufficient to overcome that which he had at his command. Provided such a force were furnished him, Coroner Smith expressed his readiness to serve the writ and release the prisoner. The necessity of this condition was apparent, and Mr. Sewall with his coadjutor proceeded to take measures for obtaining the required aid.

Under the circumstances, the ordinary posse comitatus was out of the question; for it was not to be expected that an undisciplined throng of civilians would be able to make head against the serried ranks and balls and bayonets of the Marshal's United States troops. The two gentlemen, therefore, repaired to the State House for the purpose of obtaining, if possible, a military force through the intervention of the Governor, Emory Washburn. They met him, by chance, in the office of

the Secretary of State, and at once made known
the object of their visit.   Without informing him
that a writ of replevin had actually been issued,
they put the case by supposition.   A coroner of
the city, they said, was ready to undertake the service of such a writ, provided he could be sustained
by a proper force.   They asked, therefore, whether
the Governor could not order out a sufficient number of the militia to enable him to do so.   In reply,
the Governor first reminded them of the singular
spectacle which would be presented to the world if
he were to comply with the request.   The militia
were already under arms, by order of the Mayor of
Boston, to keep the peace and suppress any
attempt, by a popular outbreak, to wrest Burns
from the custody of the United States Marshal:
was it seemly for the Governor, he inquired, to
command the same militia to aid one of the state
officers in taking him by force from the same custody?   Aside from this view of the case, he said
that while he was willing to do anything in his
power to aid their wishes, he thought that the officer to whom the writ might be committed, was
invested by the statute with all necessary power to
summon to his aid the posse comitatus.   But he
doubted whether he had authority to order out
troops to aid in serving a particular precept, unless
a case of threatened violence or actual breach of
the peace could be made out, sufficient to call into
exercise the general power confided to the Com-
mander-in-chief for such an exigency.   He then

read the provisions of the statute upon the subject, and asked Mr. Sewall whether he, as a lawyer, considered that the Governor had authority to call out troops for the express purpose of executing the writ in question. To this Mr. Sewall replied that he had looked at the matter, himself, and had great doubts if the Governor had the authority. But he added that in his view the fugitive slave act was unconstitutional, and that, consequently, the detention of Burns by the Marshal was unlawful. In answer to this, the Governor said, that whatever might be his private opinion on that point, he had been taught to regard the judiciary as the interpreters of the law; that he understood the courts to hold the law to be constitutional; and that therefore he felt bound, in his official relations, to regard it as such.

Mr. Sewall now raised a different question. By the statute providing for the writ of replevin, no person could enjoy its benefit who was "in the custody of a public officer of the law by the force of a lawful warrant or other process, civil or criminal, issued by a court of competent jurisdiction." Burns was in the custody of the United States Marshal by virtue of a Commissioner's warrant. Mr. Sewall did not regard the Commissioner as a court of competent jurisdiction, and consequently held that Burns was entitled to the writ. But the Governor, planting himself on the decisions of the Supreme Court, held that the warrant was lawful, and that Burns could not be properly interfered with while in the Marshal's custody. Yielding for the moment to this view of the case, Mr. Sewall now inquired if the Governor would order out troops to aid in serving the writ, after Burns, by virtue of the Commissioner's certificate, should have passed out of the Marshal's custody and before he should have been removed from the State? To this question, which was substantially the same as that which Coroner Smith had propounded to the City Solicitor, it does not appear that the Governor returned any specific answer, nor was it important that he should. Mr. Sewall was satisfied, on a subsequent examination of the fugitive slave act, that the Commissioner's certificate would not give Suttle the immediate possession of Burns, but that he would remain in the custody of the Marshal without any interval until he should be surrendered in Virginia. No opportunity, therefore, would be afforded for serving the writ upon Suttle within the jurisdiction of Massachusetts.

Having delivered his own views on the subject, the Governor proposed that Mr. Sewall and his coadjutor should lay the case before the Attorney-General, John H. Clifford, the legal adviser of the Executive. If that officer were able to suggest any lawful mode in which he could aid in serving the writ, he was ready to adopt it. Here the interview ended. Mr. Sewall at once sought the Attorney-General; but, not finding him readily, desisted from further pursuit, in the conviction that his opinion would be of an adverse character.[1]

The conduct of the Governor in this affair was subjected, at the time, to severe animadversion. But those who blamed him most were least informed respecting the facts. Mr. Sewall, who, as one of the parties, was familiar with all the circumstances, acquitted and justified him. With the opinions which the Governor entertained respecting his constitutional obligations, there was, Mr. Sewall thought, no other course for him to pursue. There, however, the justification stopped. The conduct might be justified by the opinions of the Governor, but the opinions themselves were condemned.

It has been seen that the Governor felt bound, whatever his private opinions or predilections, to defer to the authority of the Supreme Court. A more comprehensive survey of the action of that Court would have furnished him with equal authority for an opposite line of conduct. The particular decision upon which he rested was that in the case of Sims. But there was an earlier judgment of the Court, which, in the opinion of eminent jurists, furnished ample sanction for the application of the writ of replevin to persons in

---

[1] A little later in the day, John A. Andrew, a member of the Suffolk Bar, waited on the Governor for the same purpose, but on learning of the interview with the other gentlemen and its result, he did not press the matter. The Governor received no other application of any sort on the subject.

precisely the predicament of Burns.   This opinion
was directly connected with the restoration of
the writ of personal replevin to the statute book,
in 1837.   The committee of the legislature which
reported the bill restoring the writ, also made an
elaborate report on the general subject of the trial
by jury in questions of personal freedom.   In this
report the opinion of the Court was cited, and its
vital bearing upon the question, whether a person
arrested as a fugitive slave was entitled to the writ
of replevin, was illustrated in the comments of the
committee.   Very pertinently, the opinion had its
origin in the arrest of a fugitive slave.   One,
Griffith, had been indicted for an assault on a negro
named Randolph.   In his defence, he alleged that
Randolph was his slave, and that, by virtue of the
fugitive slave law of 1793, he had a right to seize
him.   In their reply, the prosecuting officers presented arguments against the validity of that law.
The Chief Justice, Parker, in giving his opinion,
thus disposed of them: " It is said that the act
which is passed on this subject is contrary to the
amendment of the Constitution securing the people in their persons and property against seizures,
&c., without a complaint on oath, &c.   It is very
obvious that *slaves are not parties to the Constitution, and the amendment has relation to the parties.
*   *   *   *   But it is objected that a person may, in
this summary manner, seize a freeman.   It may be
so, but it would be attended with mischievous consequences to the person making the seizure, and a
habeas corpus would lie to obtain the release of the*

person seized." And if a habeas corpus, said the
committee, then of course the concurrent remedies,
including the writ of personal replevin.

" The principle here stated," observed the committee, " when carried out relieves the act of Congress (the act of 1793) of all its obnoxious features,
and places the question, *under the law*, precisely
where the committee would have placed it, *under the
constitution*, without the law. It holds that the
proceedings are constitutional as to *slaves*, and unconstitutional as to *freemen*, and gives the person
seized, the right to try the question as to his character, by any suitable independent process. And
this principle must extend to his situation, either
before or after the certificate, for the jurisdiction
of the magistrate, upon the same reasoning, must
be special and limited, depending entirely for its
foundation upon the fact whether the person so
seized be a slave; for if he be not, the whole proceedings are void, as against the express provisions
of the constitution. It makes, then, the claimant
act at his peril throughout, and gives the person
seized an opportunity to try, in another form, the
applicability of the process to him, and that, too,
wherever he chooses."

The committee therefore expressed the opinion
that " whether the law be considered unconstitutional on the one hand, or valid on the other, upon
the construction recognized by the Supreme Court
of the Commonwealth, the same result must be
arrived at. In either case, a person seized under
the act of Congress, before or after certificate given,

may have an independent process, under which he can try his right to the character of a freeman." In concluding their report, the committee remarked, in view of the fact that the writ of personal replevin might be used by persons arrested as fugitive slaves in the investigation of their claim to freedom, that " they looked to that use of the writ as one of its just and legitimate offices." [1]

The court's opinion and the committee's interpretation of it had reference to the fugitive slave act of 1793. But they were equally applicable to the fugitive slave act of 1850, for they asserted the general principle that no act of Congress could deprive a person of his constitutional right to try the question of his freedom. Accepting this exposition, planting himself by the side, deferring to the venerable authority, of Chief Justice Parker and his associates on the Supreme Bench, the Governor might have said to Mr. Sewall: " Burns is entitled by the constitution and the law to the writ of personal replevin. Make your writ and bid the officer serve it upon the United States Marshal forthwith. If he refuses to obey, let the officer summon the posse comitatus and enforce the service. If the Marshal resists with the military force under his command, the case will have arisen in which it becomes the duty of the Governor by law to act. Then make your appli-

[1] Report of the Judiciary Committee " on the trial by jury in questions of personal freedom " made to the Massachusetts House of Representatives, March 27, 1837. The author of the report was James C. Alvord.

cation to me, and I will call out troops to aid in enforcing the writ." [1]

The interview with the Governor took place on Monday, the twenty-ninth. Nothing further was done respecting the writ until the following Wednesday. By that time the prisoner's case had assumed an unexpectedly favorable aspect. It was anticipated that the Commissioner would set him at liberty. In such a case threats had been made that Suttle would seize him again without warrant and carry him off. [2] To meet this contingency (and no other), a writ of replevin was made on that day and placed in the hands of Coroner Smith. The contingency did not occur, and the writ remained as waste paper in the officer's possession. [3]

---

[1] The whole argument may be briefly stated thus : 1. The fugitive slave acts of 1793 and 1850 are commensurate as to "competent jurisdiction." 2. The constitutionality of both has been affirmed by the Supreme Court in two different decisions. 3. The right of the person seized, to an independent trial of the question of his character, is affirmed in the first decision and not denied in the second. 4. The writ of personal replevin was provided by the Commonwealth expressly to secure such a trial; therefore, 5. The affirmation of the constitutionality of the fugitive slave act of 1850 is no bar to the use of the writ of personal replevin for the purpose of determining the character of the person seized as a slave.

[2] Suttle had resolved, *under the advice of District Attorney Hallett,* if the Commissioner's decision should be adverse to his claim, to seize Burns by force, remove him from the State, and for justification of the act rely on his ability to prove ownership after getting back to Virginia. This purpose was announced by Suttle, on the morning of June 1, to a circle of his southern friends at the Revere House, and in the hearing of the Rev. M. D. Conway, of Washington, who subsequently stated the fact to Charles M. Ellis, Esq., of Boston, and the Rev. George E. Ellis, of Charlestown.

[3] See Appendix B.

CHAPTER IV.

THE rising anger of the people filled the claimant's counsel with dismay. They feared for their own personal safety. They went constantly armed; one of them even attempted a sort of disguise. Avoiding the thronged thoroughfares, they stole to and from the Court House through the most unfrequented streets. The attack on the Court House, with the death of Batchelder, wrought their fears to a still higher pitch. It showed them that there was a band of men ready for the most desperate service that might be necessary. It prophesied fearfully of the future. What would ensue if the fugitive were surrendered? Surrendered, they at least were well assured he would be. Foreseeing this result, and taking counsel of their fears, they now resolved to avert the threatening tempest by offering Burns for sale. Thus, it was with Col. Suttle and his advisers that this proposal originated.[1]

---

[1] Colonel Suttle, despite the endorsement of his courage by Virginia, implied in his military title, appears to have been thrown into a state of extreme terror by the angry demonstrations which he had provoked. For greater personal security, he changed his quarters, in the Revere House, from a lower story to the attic, barricaded his door at night, and kept under pay four armed men to lodge with him in the room and guard him from danger. The demonstrations

6 (61)

The first announcement of this purpose was made in open court on Saturday morning. The counsel for Burns had moved for a postponement of the examination, for the purpose of gaining a little time to prepare the defence. To this the counsel for Suttle objected.

" Let the examination proceed now," said one of them, Edward G. Parker, " and if Burns is given up, I am authorized to say that he can be purchased."

Among those who heard this statement, was one who had already done and suffered much in behalf of fugitive slaves. This man was the Rev. L. A. Grimes, the pastor of a congregation of colored persons in Boston. Approaching the counsel, Mr. Grimes inquired upon what authority the statement had been made. " Col. Suttle has agreed to sell Burns," was the reply. Mr. Parker added that the sum which he had agreed to accept was twelve hundred dollars. But a condition annexed was, that the sale should be made *after* the surrender had been decreed. Mr. Grimes inquired if Col. Suttle would not consent to receive the sum named and close a bargain before the surrender. The counsel thought not. Bent on securing this concession,

which so excited his fears, proceeded chiefly from the colored men of the city. For example, four or five powerful fellows maintained an unceasing watch on a street corner, which commanded a view of his window, and never left the spot while he was known to be in the house, except to give place to a fresh set. It was afterward confessed that this expedient was adopted merely to intimidate the Colonel, and it seems to have been quite successful.

Mr. Grimes sought an interview with the Marshal, by whom, on mentioning his object, he was referred to Col. Suttle. An introduction of the slave-rescuer to the slave-hunter took place, and a long conversation ensued. Suttle enlarged on the fact of his ownership, on the kindness with which he had treated Burns, and also on the latter's good character. But to all suggestions for a sale before the surrender, he refused to listen. A private interview between Suttle and his counsel followed. At the close of it, the latter sought Mr. Grimes and informed him that their client had at length agreed to sell his slave *before* the surrender was made. The prompt response of Mr. Grimes was— "Between this time and ten o'clock to-night, I 'll have the money ready for you; have the emancipation papers ready for me at that hour."

A busy day's work lay before the benevolent pastor. The morning was already well advanced, and before the day closed, twelve hundred dollars were to be raised, not one of which had yet been subscribed. Without resources himself, he had to seek out others who might be disposed to contribute to the enterprise. A wealthy citizen, whose sympathies had hitherto been on the side of the fugitive slave act, had been heard to say that if Burns could be purchased he would head the subscription list with a hundred dollars. Informed of this by Suttle's counsel, Mr. Grimes called at the gentleman's house, and on the third attempt succeeded in finding him. The gentleman admitted that he had made the pledge already mentioned, but he now declined to redeem it. He had since met a person, he said, who had assured him that the slave could not be purchased, — that he must be tried.

" I have heard no one take that ground but the United States District Attorney," said Mr. Grimes.

The gentleman confessed that it was Attorney Hallett who had dissuaded him from acting upon his benevolent impulse. Without money, but with a promise from him to give "something," which was never redeemed, Mr. Grimes left the house.

He now bent his steps toward the mansion of a gentleman distinguished for his immense wealth, his rare munificence, and the eminent position which he had formerly held in the service of his country abroad. Everything conspired to ally him with the conservative class of society, and it was with them that public opinion commonly ranked him. What view he would take of the passing events was uncertain. Mr. Grimes found him in an unusually discomposed frame of mind. The announcement of his errand at once called forth an emphatic expression of sentiment and feeling. He denounced the fugitive slave act as " an infamous statute," and declared that he would have nothing to do with it. It had been the cause of bloodshed and slaughter, and would be the cause of still more. Referring to the death of Batchelder, he intimated that, as the man had been killed while voluntarily assisting to execute an infamous law, he had no regrets to express at the occurrence.   He could give no money to purchase the freedom of Burns, as that, in his view, would be an implied sanction of the law; but, if Mr. Grimes needed any money for his own uses, he might draw on him for the required sum, or even for a larger amount.[1] Thus encouraged, Mr. Grimes took his leave.

A gentleman belonging to a family distinguished for its ability, and especially for its devotion to the fugitive slave law, was next applied to.   At once intimating his readiness to contribute to the proposed purchase, he suggested that his brother, a wealthy merchant, should be summoned for the same purpose.   The latter soon made his appearance and entered heartily into the scheme.   Each subscribed one hundred dollars on condition that the whole sum should be raised.   Both were urgent in pressing forward the matter; "the man," said one of them, "must be out of the Court House to-night."   If the sum should not be made up, he was ready to increase his subscription. From another distinguished citizen the sum of fifty dollars was obtained; he was the only member of the national legislature from Massachusetts who had perilled his reputation by voting for the fugitive slave bill.   A subscription was next soli-

[1] The above was written while ABBOTT LAWRENCE was yet living. Now that death has set his seal on all his acts and opinions, I need no longer hesitate to name him as the person alluded to.   Let the sentiments expressed in the text go forth to the public under the sanction of such a name.

6*

cited from a certain rich broker in State street. He
had been an ardent supporter of the fugitive act;
on the occasion of sending Sims back into slavery
he had offered five thousand dollars, if need were,
to secure that triumph. Mr. Grimes now found
him in a different mood. He would give nothing
to purchase Burns — there would be no end to
demands of that sort; but he would readily contribute one hundred dollars, he said, to procure a
coat of tar and feathers for the slave-catchers.
Apparently, his patriotism cost him nothing on
either occasion. Another millionaire of the city,
who enjoyed a reputation for liberality, upon being
solicited to subscribe, declined on the ground that
it would only furnish an inducement for slaveholders to repeat their reclamations. At the same
time, he declaimed with great bitterness against the
law.

Hamilton Willis, a broker in State street, responded to the call with the most active sympathy.
He urged Mr. Grimes to obtain pledges for the
necessary amount, and agreed to advance the
money upon those pledges. Another noble contri-
butor was one who, as a Trustee of the Emigrant
Aid Society, afterward distinguished himself in
peopling Kansas with freemen. This was J. M.
S. Williams, a native of Virginia, but then a merchant in Boston. Subscribing at once a hundred
dollars, he gave assurance that whatever sum might
be deficient in the end, he would make good.

Smaller amounts were subscribed by various other persons.

At seven o'clock in the evening, Mr. Grimes had obtained pledges for eight hundred dollars. Repairing to the office of the United States Marshal, he there, according to appointment, met Mr. Willis. The latter at once filled up his cheque for the eight hundred dollars and placed it in the hands of the Marshal, to be applied toward the purchase of Burns. The counsel of Suttle had also agreed to meet Mr. Grimes at the same time and place, but they failed to make their appearance. The truth was, that, in the excess of their anxiety to have the purchase of Burns effected, one of them had undertaken to solicit subscriptions himself, and was still absent on that business.

Again Mr. Grimes went forth, — this time in company with a well known philanthropist, — and several hours were spent in fruitless endavors to make up the required amount. Late in the evening, they drove to the Revere House, where Col. Suttle had taken rooms. Soon after, the two gentlemen who acted as his counsel arrived there also. One of them now informed Mr. Grimes that he had called on the two brothers already spoken of as being so eager for the purchase of Burns, from one of whom he had received a cheque for four hundred dollars additional to his previous subscription. This was a temporary advance, however, made for the purpose of consummating the transaction within the time prescribed by Col. Suttle, and to be refunded on the following Monday. The required sum was thus completed, and nothing remained but to execute the bill of sale.

It was now half-past ten o'clock. Another half hour was consumed by a private interview between Suttle and his counsel. The several parties then separated to meet immediately after, at the private office of Commissioner Loring, with whom one of Suttle's counsel had already made an arrangement to draw up the instrument of sale. The Commissioner soon made his appearance, and at once proceeded to write a bill of sale, in these words :

" Know all men by these presents, that I, Charles F. Suttle, of Alexandria in Virginia, in consideration of twelve hundred dollars to me paid, do hereby release and discharge, quitclaim and convey to Antony Byrne[1] his liberty; and I hereby manumit and release him from all claims and service to me forever, hereby giving him his liberty to all intents and effects forever. In testimony whereof I have hereunto set my hand and seal, this twenty-seventh day of May, in the year of our Lord eighteen hundred and fifty-four."

Having completed this instrument, the Commissioner sent a messenger to Marshal Freeman, requesting his attendance at the office of the former. The Marshal declined to comply with this request.

---

[1] The name has been variously spelt; as the slave of Col. Suttle he was probably known by the name given in the bill of sale. But by his baptism of suffering he took the name of Anthony Burns, and under that designation entered upon his new life of freedom.

Mr. Loring then gathered up his papers, and, with the other parties, proceeded to the Marshal's office, where they found that official in company with District Attorney Hallett.   He at once began to confer with the Marshal concerning the purchase of Burns, when Hallett interposed and strenuously objected to the transaction.   He maintained that if Burns were, by purchase, taken out of the hands of the United States officers, before the examination were concluded, nobody would be responsible for the expenses already incurred; and he took it upon him to add that the Government would not defray them.   To this the Commissioner replied by reading a portion of the fugitive slave act.   That, he contended, made the Government responsible for the expenses; by the sale, Suttle would obtain an equivalent for his slave, and thus the law would be substantially enforced.   This absurd objection having been thus silenced, the District Attorney was ready with another.   There was, he said, an existing law of Massachusetts, which prohibited such a transaction.   The Commissioner promptly replied that the law referred to was not applicable to the case in hand; that it was a law aimed not against selling a man into freedom, but against selling him into slavery.[1]   As Mr. Hallett was not

[1] The statute referred to, I presume, was this : " Every person who shall sell, or in any manner transfer for any term, *the service or labor* of any negro, mulatto, or other person of color who shall have been unlawfully seized, taken, inveigled, or kidnapped from this State to any other State, place, or country, shall be punished by imprison-

required to be a party to the transaction, his concern on this point seemed to be somewhat gratuitous. Failing to produce conviction by arguments of this character, as a last resort he urged that the sale, if effected then, would not be legal, as the Sabbath had already commenced.   Glancing toward the clock, the Commissioner saw that the minute-hand pointed to a quarter past twelve.   He ceased to urge the point further, and, turning to Mr. Grimes, said: " It can be done at eight o'clock on Monday morning — come to my office then, and it can be settled in five minutes."   The negotiations were then broken off.

Mr. Grimes turned away in deep disappointment.   So confident was he of success, that he had a carriage in waiting at the door of the Court House to bear Burns away as a freeman.   The prisoner had been apprised of the movement in his behalf, and with feverish interest was momently waiting for his release.   Mr. Grimes now asked permission to communicate to him the result of the negotiations, and thus relieve him of a most painful suspense; but the Marshal refused his consent, at the same time charging himself with the duty.

As the Sabbath wore on, rumors spread through the city that dispatches unfavorable to the release of the prisoner had been received from the Federal

ment in the State Prison not more than ten years, or by a fine not exceeding one thousand dollars and imprisonment in the county jail not more than two years."—*Revised Statutes of Massachusetts, Chap.* 125, *Sec.* 20.

Government. Full of fears, Mr. Grimes sought an interview, at evening, with the Commissioner, at his private residence. The latter endeavored to re-assure him. Col. Suttle, he still felt confident, would abide by his agreement. " But if he fails to," said the Commissioner, " and the counsel for the defence can raise a single doubt, Burns shall walk out of the Court House a free man." He closed the interview by renewing the appointment to meet at eight o'clock, the next morning, for completing the purchase.

Punctual at the hour, Mr. Grimes repaired to the Commissioner's office, but the latter failed to appear. After waiting an hour, he went in pursuit of the delinquent functionary, but without success. He then sought Col. Suttle and his counsel at the Revere House; they were not there. At length he found them, together with Brent, Hallett, and the Marshal, assembled in the office of the latter. Reminding them of the appointment they had broken, he announced his readiness to complete the contract which had already been verbally made. Then Col. Suttle proceeded to vindicate his Virginian honor. As the bargain had not been completed on Saturday night, he said he should now decline to sell Burns; the trial must go on.

" After Burns gets back to Virginia," he graciously added, " you can then have him."

In vain Mr. Grimes urged that the failure on Saturday night occurred through no fault of his. Mr. Hallett here interrupted him.

" No," said he, " when Burns has been tried and carried back to Virginia and the law executed, you can buy him; and then I will pay one hundred dollars towards his purchase."

Mr. Grimes insisted that by agreement the man was already his. The District Attorney then said:

" The laws of the land cannot be trampled upon. A man has been killed; that blood" — pointing to the spot in the Marshal's office where Batchelder had breathed his last — "must be atoned for." Mr. Hallett thus assumed a responsibility from which he afterward, through the public press, vainly endeavored to escape.

Baffled and despondent, Mr. Grimes turned away and sought those who had subscribed to the purchase fund. He first met that supporter of the fugitive slave act who had manifested such anxiety for the release of Burns on Saturday, and who had subscribed a hundred dollars. " If the man is to be tried," said this subscriber, " I refuse to give a cent for his purchase; I would rather give five hundred dollars than have the trial go on." It was not the well-being of the slave that he sought; it was to save Boston from the ignominy arising from the execution of the fugitive slave act. Other subscribers took substantially the same position, and thus the subscription fell to the ground. Some further attempts to effect the purchase were made, in which the philanthropic broker, Mr. Willis, bore the principal share. The story of his efforts and their result is best given in his own words.

" Tuesday morning," he writes, " I had an interview with Col. Suttle in the United States Marshal's office. He seemed disposed to listen to me,
and met the subject in a manly way. He said he
wished to take the boy [Burns] back, after which
he would sell him. He wanted to see the result of
the trial at any rate. I stated to him that we considered his claim to Burns clear enough, and that he
would be delivered over to him, urging particularly
upon him that the boy's liberation was not sought
for except with his free consent, and his claim
being fully satisfied. I urged upon him no consideration of the fear of a rescue, or possible unfavorable result of the trial to him, but offered
distinctly, if he chose, to have the trial proceed, and
whatever might be the result, still to satisfy his
claim. I stated to him that the negotiation was
not sustained by any society or association whatsoever, but that it was done by some of our most
respectable citizens, who were desirous not to
obstruct the operation of the law, but in a peaceable
and honorable manner sought an adjustment of
this unpleasant case; assuring him that this feeling
was general among the people. I read to him a
letter addressed to me by a highly esteemed citizen,
urging me to renew my efforts to accomplish this,
and placing at my disposal any amount of money
that I might deem necessary for the purpose.

" Col. Suttle replied that he appreciated our
motives, and that he felt disposed to meet us. He
then stated what he would do. I accepted his

proposal at once; it was not entirely satisfactory
to me, but yet, in view of his position as he
declared to me, I was content.   At my request, he
was about to commit our agreement to writing,
when Mr. B. F. Hallett entered the office, and
they two engaged in conversation apart from me.
Presently Col. Suttle returned to me, and said 'I
must withdraw what I have done with you.'   We
both immediately approached Mr. Hallett, who
said, pointing to the spot where Mr. Batchelder
fell, in sight of which we stood, — ' That blood
must be avenged.'   I made some pertinent reply,
rebuking so extraordinary a speech, and left the
room.

"On Friday (June 2d), soon after the decision
had been rendered, finding Col. Suttle had gone on
board the cutter [which was to carry Burns back
to Virginia] at an early hour, I waited upon his
counsel at the Court House, and there renewed
my proposition.   Both these gentlemen promptly
interested themselves in my purpose, which was
to tender the claimant full satisfaction, and receive
the surrender of Burns from him, either there, in
State street, or on board the revenue cutter, at his
own option.   It was arranged between us that Mr.
Parker [junior counsel for Suttle] should go at
once on board the cutter and make an arrangement, if possible, with the Colonel.   I provided
ample funds, and returned immediately to the
Court House, when I found that there would be
difficulty in getting on board the cutter.   Applica-

tion was made by me to the Marshal; he interposed no objection, and I offered to place Mr.
Parker alongside the vessel.   Presently Mr. Parker
took me aside, and said these words : ' Col. Suttle
has pledged himself to Mr. Hallett that he will not
sell his boy until he gets him home.   Thus the
matter ended."[1]

When Burns was fairly out to sea, on his way
back to Virginia, and beyond the reach of immediate aid, the officers of the division of Massachusetts militia that had assisted in enforcing his rendition, also made an effort toward procuring his
emancipation.   Assembling at one of their ward
houses, they formally organized themselves into a
meeting, and unanimously raised a committee to
obtain funds for the purchase of Burns.   Their
purpose took a still more definite shape : jealous
for the honor of their military body, they voted
that the subscription should be strictly confined to
the officers and members of their division.   Un-
happily, this was the end, as well as the beginning,
of their efforts.   The cause of the failure, as afterwards assigned by some of their number, was the
severe criticism with which their participation in
the surrender had been treated by the public press.
Finding that the proposed benefaction was not
likely to efface from the public mind the remem-

---

[1] Letter of Hamilton Willis, addressed to the Editors of the Boston
Atlas and published in that journal, June 5, 1854, in reply to Mr.
Hallett's public denial of the charge that he had interfered to pre-
vent the purchase of Burns.

brance of their previous official conduct, they abandoned their purpose and prudently reserved their money.

In time, news reached Boston that Burns had arrived in Virginia. The law had been executed, the point of honor had been satisfied, Slavery had its own again. Negotiations were once more renewed. At the request of Mr. Grimes, Mr. Willis addressed a letter to Col. Suttle on the subject. The reply of the latter is entitled to a place in this history.

"I have had much difficulty in my own mind," he writes, "as to the course I ought to pursue about the sale of my man, Anthony Burns, to the North. Such a sale is objected to strongly by my friends, and by the people of Virginia generally, upon the ground of its pernicious character, inviting our negroes to attempt their escape under the assurance that, if arrested and remanded, still the money would be raised to purchase their freedom. As a southern man and a slave-owner, I feel the force of this objection and clearly see the mischief that may result from disregarding it. Still, I feel no little attachment to Anthony, which his late elopement, [with] the vexation and expense to which I have been put, has not removed; and I confess to some disposition to see the experiment tried of bettering his condition.

"I understand the application now made to purchase his freedom, does not come from the abolitionists and incendiaries who put the laws of the Union at defiance, and dyed their hands in the blood of Batchelder, but from those who struggled to maintain law and order.

" Now that the laws have been fully vindicated (although at the point of the bayonet) and Anthony returned to the city of Richmond, from which he escaped; and believing that it would materially strengthen the Federal Officers and facilitate the execution of the laws in any future case which might arise, and influenced by other considerations to which I have referred, I have concluded to sell him his freedom for the sum of fifteen hundred dollars.

" When in Boston, acting under the extraordinary counsel of Mr. Parker, one of my lawyers, I agreed to take twelve hundred dollars if paid at a fixed period. The money was not forthcoming at the time agreed upon,[1] and I then, being better advised, determined the law should take its course.

" By the course pursued of violent, corrupt, and perjured opposition to my rights, the case was pro·tracted for days after my offer to take twelve hundred dollars ; consequently my expenses were generally increased, I presume materially so to my attorneys, to whom I paid from my private purse four hundred dollars.[2]

[1] This was not true, as the narrative in the former part of this chapter shows.

[2] The excuse which Col. Suttle here presents for his exorbitant demand for Burns will hardly stand a severe scrutiny. According to his own admission, he had agreed to accept twelve hundred dollars. Afterward, acting under "better advice," he withdrew his

7*

" Now, as I am not a man of wealth, and I am bound to have a moderate regard for my private interest, it will readily be seen that twelve hundred dollars at the time I agreed to take it, would have been better for me than fifteen hundred now.

" In reply to your question about his (Burns,) character, I have to say that I regard him as strictly honest, sober, and truthful. Let me hear from you without delay. If you accede to my terms, I will, on receipt of the money, deliver him in the city of Washington with his free papers, or I will send him by one of the steamers from Richmond to New York."

With this new proposition, the indefatigable pastor, Grimes, sought first of all Mr. Hallett, and, informing him of its nature, plainly told the attorney that, as he was the only one who had hindered the purchase of Burns at twelve hundred dollars, he alone ought to bear the burden of the excess now demanded over that sum. Hallett refused to grace himself by such an act of justice, but, nevertheless, declared his willingness to give a hundred dollars toward the sum required. Col. Suttle's proposition was next laid before the persons who had acted as

---

offer for the purpose of letting the law take its course. The law did take its course, and an increase of his expenses was the natural result. The proposed purchasers were anxious to have him take a step that would diminish his expenses; he insisted on pursuing a course which he knew would increase them, and then, because they were increased, required that the purchasers should bear the burden. It furnishes some relief to one's sense of justice to know that he was afterwards obliged to go farther and fare worse.

his counsel. They addressed a letter to him, declaring it as their opinion that he was bound to accept twelve hundred dollars for Burns ; but nothing came of this remonstrance. Mr. Grimes then applied to the original subscribers to the twelve hundred dollar fund. Most of them were ready to renew their pledges, provided Burns could be purchased for that amount; but they absolutely refused to give anything if a higher sum were insisted on. Col. Suttle was then informed by Mr. Grimes that he could still have the twelve hundred dollars, but nothing more. To this no answer was ever returned, and for the time all efforts to ransom Burns were at an end.

CHAPTER V.

THE EXAMINATION.

THE examination in due form commenced on Monday, the twenty-ninth of May. Court Square presented on that morning a strange and alarming scene in free Massachusetts. There was nothing to indicate that a solemn judicial proceeding was about to take place. The Court House, an immense pile of stone, resembling, in its massive strength, a donjon keep of the middle ages, wore the air of a beleaguered fortress. At the windows in different stories of the building, the mingled soldiery of Massachusetts and of the United States presented themselves, with firearms, as at the embrasures of a rampart. Below, a vast throng of citizens, which had been constantly increasing from early dawn, surged around the base of the building and through the spacious Square in unappeasable excitement. All the outer entrances of the Court House had been securely closed, except one at which was stationed a strong force of the police. Even here, none were allowed to enter but the functionaries, the reporters for the press, and a few citizens who, by special favor, had obtained per-

(80)

mits from the Marshal.[1] Once within the walls,
it was not certain that the adventurous citizen
would be able to make his way to the tribunal.
At the foot of the stairs leading to the court-room,
files of soldiers barred the passage with their muskets, and raised them only at the nod of a custom-
house officer deputed for the service. On the first
landing-place were stationed more soldiers with
fixed bayonets, and others still, at the head of the
stairs. So strictly was the guard maintained, that
those who had passed the first sentries were, in
some instances, arrested and detained upon the
stairway by the last. And not until the last
moment before the opening of the court, were any
except the officials, allowed to pass. Never before,
in the history of Massachusetts, had the avenues
to a tribunal of justice been so obstructed by serried bayonets borne in the hands of an alien and
mercenary soldiery.

The court-room was not spacious, but it more
than sufficed to contain those who were suffered to
enter it. Many seats remained vacant as silent
witnesses to the excessive fears of those who had
enlisted in this enterprise against the popular feel-

---

[1] In some instances, citizens of Massachusetts were excluded, while
citizens of southern states were readily admitted.   Charles G. Davis,
Esq., of Plymouth, a well known lawyer, applied for admission in
company with a friend.   The latter was allowed to pass, on being
introduced as "a gentleman from Washington, D. C.;" but Mr.
Davis was kept out, and furthermore, was told by the underlings
that they had orders to exclude him and all other "free-soilers."
As a member of the Massachusetts Bar he had a *right* to enter.

ing. Of those who were present, the most conspicuous, if not the most numerous portion, were
pimps and bullies, whose vile passions and brutal
natures had left a permanent impress upon their
persons.   Some of them, now appearing as officers
of justice, were convicted criminals and had served
out their sentence in the prisons. These carried it
boldly, as though they had been presented with the
freedom of the court-room ; while the few good
citizens present, — some, men of substance, and
some, men of renown, — took their seats quietly
as being conscious that they were there on suffer-
ance.   Nothing, perhaps, more clearly revealed the
nature of the business in hand than the fact that
the Marshal was compelled to rely for aid, chiefly,
on the most depraved class of men in the community.

At length the court was opened.   Alone, upon
the bench from which Judge Story had been wont
to dispense justice, sat the Commissioner, evidently
oppressed by the load which he had chosen to take
upon himself.   In his appropriate place on the
right stood the Marshal, Watson Freeman, in
whose massy face, seamed by small pox, a certain
look of good humor somewhat modified the prevailing relentlessness of its aspect.   Over against
the Commissioner, upon a seat just without the
bar, sat Anthony Burns.   On either side of him,
as guards, sat two or three brutal-looking men, and
in front of him, just within the bar, were four or
five more, with pistols and bludgeons lurking in

their pockets and but half concealed from the offended eyes of the spectators. At the clerk's desk, apart, sat the United States District Attorney, Benjamin F. Hallett, whose business there did not clearly appear. The counsel for the slaveholder and the slave respectively, the reporters for the press, the slaveholder and his southern friends, Theodore Parker, the Rev. L. A. Grimes, Morris, the colored lawyer of Boston, and some few others occupied the seats within the bar; while a moderate number outside completed the assemblage.

The first incident in the proceedings illustrated the character of the tribunal. Charles M. Ellis, the junior counsel for Burns, began with a protest against proceeding in the case under the extraordinary circumstances of the occasion.

" It is not fit," said he, " that we should proceed while counsel here (meaning the counsel for Suttle) bear arms. It is not fit that the prisoner should sit here with shackles on his limbs. It is not fit that we should proceed while the court-room is packed with armed men, and all the avenues to it are filled with soldiery, making it difficult for the friends of the prisoner to obtain access to him. I protest against proceeding under these circumstances."

" The examination must proceed," was the prompt response of the Commissioner. But Mr. Hallett, whose offensive and unexplained presence within the bar has already been alluded to, now joined issue, and proceeded to harangue the Com-

missioner in reply to what had been said. The
Commissioner, immediately interrupting, reminded
him that, as he had already decided the point, any
further remarks were unnecessary. The District
Attorney persisted. The conduct of the Marshal,
he said, had been called in question, and he was
present to act as his counsel. Again the Commissioner interposed: " Mr. Hallett, these remarks
are irrelevant and entirely out of order." But the
Attorney, without even pausing in his speech, went
on with raised voice, inflamed countenance, and
increased vehemence of manner, not only to repel
the reflections that had been cast upon the Marshal,
but also to instruct the Commissioner in his own
duty. Insolence triumphed, and the Commissioner
sank back in his seat with a helpless air, until the
browbeating was ended. Men who had been
wont to see the Bench treated with the profoundest
respect by the Bar, who had known Daniel Webster bow in silence and resume his seat at the bidding of a common pleas judge, looked on indignant and amazed. Why was not the Attorney
ordered into instant custody ? Had the Court no
power to protect itself ?

Another incident, that occurred at a later stage
of the examination, furnished an answer to this
question. In attempting to return to the court-
room, after one of the short recesses that were
reluctantly granted, Mr. Dana, the senior counsel
for Burns, found his progress obstructed by the
bayonets of the guard. In vain he urged his well

known relation to the prisoner; he was kept waiting upon the stairs until it was the pleasure of the Marshal to permit him to pass on. The outrage was made known to the Commissioner, and he was moved to instruct the Marshal upon the subject. " I have no authority to direct the actions of the Marshal," was the short but pregnant answer, while that officer stood grimly smiling upon the foiled advocate of Freedom. The Marshal did not sustain the relation of a sheriff to a justiciary court; he was in no wise amenable to the Commissioner. He might surround the court-room with soldiery, admit or exclude whom he pleased, subject one party in the suit to personal outrages and bestow special indulgences on the other, and there was no one to call him to account. The Commissioner was not supreme in his own court. Under this confessed state of things, the examination went forward.

The case of the claimant had already been presented, while as yet Anthony had no one to defend him ; but now, upon the demand of his counsel, the Commissioner ordered that the examination should commence anew. The complaint was read by Edward G. Parker, the junior counsel for the claimant. William Brent was then placed upon the stand. It appeared that he was a slaveholding grocer of Richmond, Virginia. He testified that he was the personal friend of Col. Suttle, and had long been acquainted with him. He had known him as a slaveholder, and as the owner of a slave

8

named Anthony Burns. He had himself hired
Anthony of Suttle for three years, and had also
acted as the latter's agent in hiring him out to one
Millspaugh. In this way he had come to have
intimate personal knowledge of Suttle's ownership
of Burns, and also of Burns' personal appearance.
He now stated that the prisoner was the same
Anthony Burns whom he had so well known in
Virginia. He further said that he had last seen
Anthony in that State on the twentieth of March,
1854; on the twenty-fourth, Anthony was missing,
and on the Tuesday following, he communicated
the fact to Col. Suttle, who was then residing in
Alexandria. But of the manner in which Burns
left Virginia he knew nothing.

The counsel for the claimant now proposed to
put in, as evidence, the admissions which Anthony
had made since his arrest.

" We object," said Mr. Ellis; " the sixth section
of the fugitive slave law provides that the evidence of the alleged fugitive shall not be taken."

" The admissions and confessions of Burns are
a very different thing from testimony," replied Seth
J. Thomas, the claimant's senior counsel; "as a
party in the suit — the defendant — he is not privileged to testify."

" It is the height of cruelty to the prisoner,"
urged Mr. Dana, " to take advantage of the only
power he has under this law — that of speech —
to his detriment, when the claimant, the other party

in the suit, has not only his own right, but, in these alleged confessions, a portion of the prisoner's."

On the decision of this question, as the result proved, hung the fate of Anthony Burns. Even at this early stage of the proceedings, before the nature of the defence was known, the important bearing of the point was discerned. A breathless silence reigned in the court-room.

" I think," said the Commissioner, " that the word 'testimony,' in the law, must be regarded as referring to evidence given by a witness, and not to confessions or admissions; but I am unwilling to prejudice the liberty of the prisoner, and his counsel may have the right to pass that question for the present."

" We desire that the questions may be asked and the answers taken down for future use, if necessary," said the claimant's counsel.

The Court assented, and the witness proceeded to relate the conversation that took place, as follows: " Burns said he did not intend to run away, but being at work on board a vessel, and getting tired, fell asleep, when the vessel sailed with him on board. On Mr. Suttle's going into the room after the arrest, the first word from Burns was, 'How do you do, Master Charles?' The next thing was, 'Did I ever whip you, Anthony?' The answer was, 'No.' The next question was, 'Did I ever hire you where you did not want to go?' The reply was, 'No.' The next question was, 'Did you ever ask me for money when it was not given you? The answer was, 'No.' Mr. Suttle then asked, 'Did I not, when you were sick, take my bed from my own house for you?' and the answer was, 'Yes.' He then recognized me, and said, 'How do you do, Master William?' Being asked substantially if he was willing to go back, he said he was." [1]

With some further unimportant details, the examination in chief was ended. A close cross-examination followed, but failed to elicit any additional evidence materially affecting the case. Throughout, the testimony of this witness was direct and unequivocal, and was delivered with an air of careless superiority, which was natural to a slaveholder testifying against a slave, and was not uncongenial to the peculiar tribunal in whose character there was nothing to overawe.

In giving in his testimony, the witness spoke of Burns and his relatives as " slaves." The counsel for Burns objected to this term. " The witness must not state any person to be a slave," said the Commissioner, " without corroborative legal evidence." This instruction from the Court caused

[1] The important discrepancies between this statement of the conversation and that given on pp. 18, 19, chap. I., will be apparent at a glance. That statement was taken down from the lips of Burns by the author of this work. Burns emphatically denied the correctness of Brent's report of the conversation, and declared his readiness to make oath to the correctness of his own. As Col. Suttle stated in writing over his own signature, after he had returned to Virginia with his recovered property, that he continued to regard Burns as " strictly truthful," the reader will have at least his sanction for believing the statement of Burns in preference to that of Brent.

not a little embarrassment to the witness. The habits of a Virginia slaveholder were inveterate upon him, and he found it difficult to extemporise forms of speech suited to the latitude of a free state and to the ears of a free people.

One, Caleb Page, a Boston truckman, was next called to corroborate Brent's testimony respecting the admissions of Burns on the night of the arrest. He had assisted in arresting the prisoner, and, according to his own statement, was "just the man wanted" by the officer for that business. His testimony added nothing to the strength of the claimant's case, and he had little reason to thank his employers for uselessly dragging him forth from obscurity to become an object of odium to his fellow citizens.

" We now propose," said the claimant's counsel, " to put in the record of the court of Virginia as evidence."

" It is in the case," said the Commissioner, " subject to objection from counsel."

The counsel for the defence examined the record. " We should have several objections to present against it," said they, " which, in the absence of a jury, we should like to present to the Court." [1]

" The record," said Mr. Parker, " is decisive of two points: first, that Burns owed service and labor, second, that he escaped." On the point of identity he requested the Commissioner to examine the marks upon the prisoner.

[1] See Appendix C.

8*

"I perceive," said the Commissoner, "the scars on the cheek and hand, and take cognizance with my eye of the prisoner's height." He offered to have the prisoner brought up for a closer examination, but this was declined.

A volume of Virginia laws relative to the organization and power of courts was presented as evidence. Objection was made.

"A *book* is here presented," said Mr. Dana, "to show that a person owes service and labor in Virginia! We deny the sufficiency of the evidence."

"The proper way," said the opposing counsel, "to prove the law of another state is by books; if the book is not sufficient, I wish to prove the fact in another way."

"Let the book go in as testimony for what it is worth," said the Commissioner.

The evidence on the part of the claimant here closed. The court had been in session five hours, and an adjournment was asked for. At first, the Commissioner refused to grant it, his anxiety to press the case to a close overpowering all considerations of judicial decorum. With great reluctance, he was at length persuaded to allow a half-hour's recess to enable the prisoner's counsel to examine authorities and make some other necessary preparation.[1]

Upon the re-assembling of the court, Mr. Ellis

[1] The greater part of this brief recess was rendered of no avail by the obstructions which the officials and the military presented in the way of the counsel for Burns.

opened for the defence. Allowed but a single day
for preparation, denied access to the law library of
the court, obstructed and delayed in his movements
by the military, he entered upon his task under the
greatest embarrassment. He and his associate
had been charged with seeking, not a trial under,
but a triumph over the law. This was denied.
" Not only," said he, " have I never sought to resist
the law, but I have done something to stay resistance to it. I stand here for the prisoner, under,
and not against the law."

The position of the prisoner was impressively
described. " Seized on a false charge, without
counsel, the prisoner is to be doomed. And then,
with no power to test jurisdiction, when every
one of the writs of the common law for personal
liberty's security is found to have failed, without
time, without food, without free access to the court,
without the show of free action or free thought
within it, without challenge for favor or bias, for
cause or without cause, without jury, without
proofs in form, or witnesses to confront him, with
a judge sitting with his hands tied, in nearly all
points the merest tool of the most monstrous of
anomalies, with no power to render a judgment,
but full power to doom to the direst sentence, I say
that in all things save one—in your opinion—the
prisoner has not the semblance of justice."

It had been urged that the examination was
merely preliminary. " They know better," replied
the advocate, " when they say so. The law looks

no further, nothing is to follow. This is the final act in the farce of hearing. They know, we know, you know, that if you send him hence with them, he goes to the block, to the sugar or cotton plantation, to the lash under which I have heard that Sims, who entered the dark portal, breathed out his life." Therefore he adjured the Commissioner to refuse the certificate of surrender except upon the most overwhelming proof.

And what proof had the claimant presented? He had called only a single witness, and had produced a written paper which he styled a record of a Virginia court. This evidence, the counsel alleged, was defective in many particulars, which he pointed out; some of it was inadmissible, and what was admissible was insufficient. The fugitive slave act was commented upon, and several positions were stated upon which it was claimed that act ought to be declared unconstitutional.

" For the reasons now presented," said the advocate, in closing his review, " the claimant shows no claim to a certificate; and, if such a case stood alone, we feel that it ought to be dismissed."

" But," continued he with altered look and voice, " the prisoner has a case of his own. The complaint alleges, the only record offered proves, the only witness called testifies to, an escape from Richmond on the twenty-fourth day of March last. The witness swears clearly and positively that he saw this prisoner in Richmond on the twentieth day of March.

" We shall call a number of witnesses to show, —fixing, as I think, the man and the time beyond question,—that the prisoner was in Boston on the first of March last, and has been here ever since up to the time of this seizure. This is our defence." An *alibi* was to be proved.[1]

A colored citizen of South Boston, named William Jones, was called upon the stand. He testified that he first saw Burns in Washington street, Boston, on the first day of March, 1854, and that on the fourth of the same month he employed him to labor in the Mattapan Works at South Boston. He was able to fix the dates by reference to a memorandum book, in which, at his request, a certain Mr. Russell had made an entry of the time, and which was produced by him in court. The particularity of detail with which this testimony was given, presented a field for attack which the claimant's counsel did not fail to improve. A sharp and protracted cross-examination followed, but it failed to shake the testimony, and, at the end of several hours, the witness was permitted to retire from the stand.

George H. Drew, a white citizen of Boston, confirmed the statements of the colored witness. He was the book-keeper at the Mattapan Works, in March; knew Jones to have been employed

[1] The word *alibi* is the one that most nearly expresses the idea sought to be conveyed. I am told that it is not in good odor with the legal profession. Let it be taken without the bad odor, and the reader will get no wrong impression.

there on the first of that month, and then saw
Burns with him. He had no doubt of the man's
identity; and he had, moreover, observed that on
his first entering the court-room, Burns had appeared to recognize him by following him round
the room with his eyes.

James F. Whittemore, a member of the city
council of Boston, and a director of the Mattapan
Works, swore that he saw Burns there on the
eighth or ninth of March, at work with Jones·
He identified the man by the scars on his cheek
and right hand, and fixed the time by reference to
his return from a journey. To a question from the
prisoner's counsel, he replied that he was an officer
of the Pulaski Guards, then under arms for the
purpose of quelling any disturbance growing out
of this affair, and that he was not a free-soiler or
abolitionist, but a hunker whig. This explanation
was fitted to increase the weight of his testimony
on the public mind.

Stephen Maddox, a colored clothing trader in
Boston, had seen Burns at his store in March, accompanied by Jones. He had particularly noticed
the mark on his cheek, and was able to say that
the time was about the first of the month.

William C. Culver, a blacksmith, H. N. Gilman,
a teamster, and Rufus A. Putnam, a machinist, all
of whom had been employed at the Mattapan
Works in March, testified with various degrees of
particularity to having seen the prisoner there before
the middle of that month.

John Favor, a carpenter, had seen Burns, accompanied by Jones, in his shop, some time between the first and fifth of March, he thought; he had no doubt that the prisoner was the man.

Finally, Horace W. Brown, a police officer, testified that, while employed as a carpenter at the Mattapan Works, he had seen Burns at work there with Jones, some week or ten days before he left, which was on the twentieth of March. He had not the slightest doubt about the man's identity.

The evidence for the prisoner was closed. As it progressed, a marked change in the countenances and manner of the claimant and his party had gradually made itself manifest. They had greeted the first colored witness with a fixed stare of contemptuous incredulity; his story they regarded as the falsehood of a perjurer, and when the ingenuity of the counsel in cross-examining proved no match for the negro's self-possession, they still looked upon it as only the case of a "lie well stuck to." The testimony of the next witness, a respectable white citizen, somewhat abated their lofty and assured looks; but when one who was clothed with the double responsibilities of civil and military office, who was at the time on duty in the claimant's behalf, and who disavowed the character of an abolitionist,— when this witness emphatically confirmed the testimony previously given, all the assurance of the claimant and his friends gave place to unfeigned anxiety and alarm, while wonder and hope played over the countenances of those who sympathized with the prisoner. Witness after witness followed, until the cumulative evidence of nine persons stood arrayed in irreconcilable hostility against the single testimony of Brent. It seemed beyond a question that the *alibi* had been established.

An effort was now made to destroy the force of the evidence in behalf of the prisoner, by the introduction of rebutting evidence. One of the witnesses, called for this purpose, had been a keeper over Burns, from the time of the arrest; he was expected to testify to certain statements made by the prisoner while in his charge. This was objected to, on the general ground that the prisoner's admissions were not to be received at all; on the further ground that, in this instance, they had been made under intimidation; and finally, on the ground that it was not rebutting testimony. Notwithstanding, the Commissioner ruled that it should be admitted. Accordingly, the witness proceeded to state that in conversation with himself, during the period of arrest, Burns had said that he had been in Boston about two months, and that previously he had been in Richmond, Virginia. With this piece of evidence from a hireling of the slaveholder, the testimony on both sides was closed.

CHAPTER VI.

Amidst the deepest silence, Richard H. Dana, Jr., rose to make the closing argument for the prisoner. The son of one of America's most eminent poets, the grandson of a Chief Justice of Massachusetts, he was less indebted to ancestral fame for the high position which he at the time enjoyed, than to his own genius and industry. Compelled, while a member of the University, to abandon the pursuit of science for the pursuit of health, he had shipped before the mast on board a vessel bound to the then almost uninhabited coast of California, for a cargo of raw hides. In this situation, sharing in all the perils and toils and pleasures of the common sailor, on ship and on shore, now out upon a yard-arm reefing sails in a tempest, now on land, day after day, bending beneath a load of filthy hides, he underwent an experience which would have rendered a coarse nature only coarser, but which, transmuted and improved by his finer nature, and afterwards given to the world in the celebrated and fascinating "Two Years Before the Mast," became the foundation of his future fortunes. Elected a member of the Convention for

9   (97)

revising the Constitution of Massachusetts in 1853, he there quickly distinguished himself, and by universal consent took his place in the first rank of that eminent body. He was now, by his generous and powerful defence of the oppressed, about to earn fresh laurels for his brow.[1] Of moderate temper, of conservative principles, of charitable judgment, he yet felt impelled, by the unparalleled circumstances of the occasion, to preface his argument with an exordium so stinging and intolerable in its truth, that the miscreants at whom it was levelled, and upon whose ears it fell, glutted their revenge, not long after, by waylaying him in the street at night and felling him to the ground.[2] Widely circulated in the papers of the day, it deserves a place upon the permanent page of history.

" I congratulate you, Sir," said he, " that your labors, so anxious and painful, are drawing to a close. I congratulate the Commonwealth of Massachusetts that she is to be relieved from that in-

[1] Two purses, of $200 each, were made up by the Committee of Vigilance, and tendered to Messrs. Dana and Ellis, but the service had been given from love of the cause, and the money was declined. Subsequently, pieces of silver plate, with suitable inscriptions, were presented to each gentleman by the same parties.

[2] One of them was arrested and put under bonds to appear for trial, but before the appointed time he fled to New Orleans. His bondsmen, irritated at his want of good faith, procured a requisition from Governor Washburn upon the Governor of Louisiana, and sent an officer in pursuit. He was apprehended, brought back, tried, and sentenced to hard labor for a term of years in the State Prison.

cubus which has rested on her for so many days
and nights, making her to dream strange dreams
and see strange visions. I congratulate her that
at length, in due time, by leave of the Marshal of
the United States, and the District Attorney of the
United States, first had and obtained therefor, her
courts may be re-opened, and her judges, suitors,
and witnesses may pass and repass without being
obliged to satisfy hirelings of the United States
Marshal and bayonetted foreigners, clothed in the
uniform of our army and navy, that they have a
right to be there. I congratulate the city of Boston that her peace here is no longer to be in danger. Yet I cannot but admit that while her peace
here is in some danger, the peace of all other parts
of the city has never been so safe as while the
Marshal has had his posse of specials in this Court
House. Why, Sir, people have not felt it necessary to lock their doors at night, the brothels are
tenanted only by women, fighting-dogs and racing-
horses have been unemployed, and Ann street and
its alleys and cellars show signs of a coming mil-
lennium.

" I congratulate, too, the Government of the
United States, that its legal representative can
return to his appropriate duties, and that his sedulous presence will no longer be needed here in a
private civil suit for the purpose of intimidation, a
purpose which his effort the day before yesterday
showed every desire to effect, which although it
did not influence this Court in the least, I deeply

regret that your Honor did not put down at once, and bring to bear upon him the judicial power of this tribunal. I congratulate the Marshal of the United States that the ordinary respectability of his character is no longer to be in danger from the character of the associates he is obliged to call about him. I congratulate the officers of the army and navy that they can be relieved from this service, which as gentlemen and soldiers surely they despise, and can draw off their non-commissioned officers and privates, both drunk and sober, from this fortified slave-pen to the custody of the forts and fleets of our country, which have been left in peril that this great Republic might add to its glories the trophies of one more captured slave."

With this introduction, Mr. Dana proceeded to his argument. The Commissioner had declared in the outset that he should presume the prisoner to be a freeman until he was proved a slave. To this declaration Mr. Dana held the Court. Upon it he rested his hopes. It was for the claimant, therefore, to furnish evidence that the prisoner was his slave. He had described a certain slave belonging to him — was the prisoner that slave? This was a question of identity. But on the point of identity men were liable to be mistaken — actually *had* been mistaken. Jacob had been mistaken for Esau by his own father. The history of slave-catching furnished examples of terrible mistakes of this sort. A freeman named Gibson had been remanded from Philadelphia to Maryland as a slave. Another named Freeman had been sent into slavery from Indiana. With such impressive instances on record, it was all important to guard against any mistake. What evidence of identity in this case had Suttle furnished? First and chiefly, there was Brent's testimony. But Brent had not been favorably situated for identifying Burns. Then, the description in the record was relied upon; but the description was loose, and the record itself was probably nothing but Brent on paper. It was further said, that Brent's liability to bias as a Virginian should be taken into consideration.

"But," continued Mr. Dana, "there is fortunately one fact of which Mr. Brent is sure. He knows that he saw this Anthony Burns in Richmond, Virginia, on the twentieth day of March last, and that he disappeared from there on the twenty-fourth. To this fact he testified unequivocally. After all the evidence is put in on our side to show that the prisoner was in Boston on the first and fifth of March, he does not go back to the stand to correct an error, or to say that he may have been mistaken, or that he only meant to say that it was *about* the twentieth or twenty-fourth. He persists in his positive testimony, and I have no doubt that he is right and honest in doing so. He did see Anthony Burns in Richmond, Virginia, on the twentieth day of March, and Anthony Burns was first missing from there on the twenty-fourth. But the prisoner was in Boston, earning an honest livelihood by the work of his hands, through the active month of

March, from the first day forward. Of this your Honor cannot, on the proofs, entertain a reasonable doubt."

Mr. Dana proceeded to review the testimony introduced by the defence on this point. The principal witness was Jones. He had sworn with great particularity of detail that the prisoner was seen by him in Boston on the first day of March, and was at work with him in his employ on the fifth and eighteenth of the same month, in the same city. He could not be mistaken respecting the man's identity. This testimony was vital, and was either the truth, or a pure fabrication. " I saw at once," said Mr. Dana, " as every one must have seen, that the story so full of details, with such minuteness of names, and dates, and places, must either stand impregnable, or be shattered to pieces. The severest test has been applied. The other side has had a day in which to follow up the points of Jones's diary, and discover his errors and falsehoods. But he is corroborated in every point."

Having passed in review the testimony of the other witnesses confirming that of Jones, the advocate proceeded to set forth the cumulative effect of such an array of witnesses. " On a question of identity," said he, " numbers are everything. One man may mistake by accident, design, or bias. His sight may be poor, his observation imperfect, his opportunities slight, his recollection of faces not vivid. But if six or eight men agree on identity, the evidence has more than six or eight times the force of one man's opinion. Each man has his own mode and means and habits of observation and recollection. One observes one thing, and another another thing. One makes this combination and association, and another that. One sees him in one light, or expression, or position, or action, and another in another. One remembers a look, another a tone, another the gait, another the gesture. Now if a considerable number of these independent observers combine upon the same man, the chances of mistake are lessened to an indefinite degree. What other man could answer so many conditions presented in such various ways? On the point of the time and the place, too, each of those witnesses is an independent observer. These are not links in one chain, each depending on another. They are separate rays, from separate sources, uniting on one point."

In concluding this part of his argument, Mr. Dana inquired: " If the burden of proof had been upon us, should we not have met it? How much more, then, are we entitled to prevail where we have only to shake the claimant's case by showing that it is left in reasonable doubt? "

A new and independent line of argument was now taken. " Throw out," said Mr. Dana, " all of our testimony and rest the case on the claimant's evidence alone." Two questions were to be met: Did the prisoner owe service to Suttle? Did he escape from Virginia into Massachusetts? The claimant offered the record of the Virginia Court

as conclusive on both these points. It was agreed
that such would be its effect if the proper mode
of proceeding was adopted. The fugitive slave
act provided two methods. By the tenth section
the questions of slavery and escape were to be
tried *ex parte*, in the state from which the person
escaped; and the record of this was to be conclusive. By the sixth section, the same questions
might be tried in the state where the escaping
person was found. These were distinct, independent methods, and the claimant was at liberty to
proceed under either. He had, however, proceeded
under both; he had attempted to prove the facts
of slavery and escape by parole and other evidence
before the Commissioner, and he had also offered
the Virginia record as conclusive of the same facts.
But this was inadmissible. The two methods
could not be thus combined. The structure of the
statute plainly implied the reverse. Having elected
to proceed under the sixth section, the claimant
was no longer at liberty to introduce his record
under the tenth.

But, if the record were considered as admissible
in other respects, and conclusive if admitted, it was
still objectionable both in form and substance. It
did not purport to be a record of the matters proved.
It did not describe the person with such convenient
certainty as might be. It did not allege that he
escaped into another state. " On one or more of
these points," said Mr. Dana, " we have great confidence that the record will be excluded, or that, if

admitted, we may control it by the claimant's own testimony."

One part of the testimony showed that Burns, at the time of his escape, owed service, not to Suttle, but to Millspaugh. He was leased to Millspaugh. This was in flat contradiction to the record. What right then had Suttle to claim Burns? Until the lease expired, Millspaugh had the sole right of possession and control. "Mr. Millspaugh," argued Mr. Dana, "may allow him to come to Massachusetts and stay here until the end of the lease, if he chooses. Col. Suttle has nothing to say about it." But this was not all. The testimony of Brent showed that Burns had been mortgaged, and there was no evidence before the Commissioner that the mortgage had been discharged. On this ground, also, Suttle was precluded from interfering.

An essential element in the claimant's case was the *escape*. Had there been any escape? There was no evidence of the fact. To constitute an escape, two things must concur: that the person came away, first, of his own will, and second, against his master's will. The claimant had introduced evidence showing that Burns had not escaped of his own will; and by that evidence he was bound. Respecting Millspaugh, his master for the time, and the only person having a right at the time to say whether he should go or come, no evidence at all had been introduced. A case of escape, then, had not been made out, and as, by the decisions of the Courts, the *escape* is the *casus fœderis* under the constitution, the prisoner could not rightfully be sent back to Virginia.

The admissions of Burns were last considered. They were made under extraordinary circumstances. The prisoner was overwhelmed with terror. They rested on the evidence of a single witness testifying under the strongest bias, and who, in regard to one part of the admissions which he swore to, had been proved to have been mistaken. But, under any circumstances, the Commissioner should have ruled them out. Reason, humanity, and precedent, required that they should not be received.

On the constitutional question, Mr. Dana said he should offer the propositions in the same form in which they were cast by Mr. Rantoul in the *Sims' case*, and not argue them at all, putting them forward as a continued protest:

I. That the power which the Commissioner is called upon in this procedure to exercise is a judicial power, and one that, if otherwise lawful, can be exercised only by a judge of the United States Court, duly appointed, and that the Commissioner is not such a judge.

II. That the procedure is a suit between the claimant and captive, involving an alleged right of property on the one hand, and the right of personal liberty on the other, and that either party, therefore, is entitled to trial by jury; and the law which purports to authorize a delivery of the captive to the claimant, denying him the privilege of such a trial, and which he here claims under judicial process, is unconstitutional and void.

III. That the transcript of testimony taken before the magistrates of a state court in Georgia, and of the judgment thereupon by such magistrates, is incompetent evidence, Congress having no power to confer upon state courts or magistrates judicial authority to determine, conclusively or otherwise, upon the effect of evidence to be used in a suit pending or to be tried in another state, or before another tribunal.

IV. That such evidence is also incompetent, because the captive was not represented at the taking thereof, and had no opportunity for cross-examination.

V. That the statute under which the process is instituted is unconstitutional and void, as not within the power granted to Congress by the Constitution, and because it is opposed to the express provisions thereof.

Mr. Dana closed with an impressive appeal to the Commissioner. "You recognized, Sir," said he, "in the beginning, the presumption of freedom. Hold to it now, Sir, as to the sheet anchor of your own peace of mind, as well as of the prisoner's safety. If you make a mistake in favor of the prisoner, a pecuniary value, not great, is put at hazard. If against him, a free man is made a slave. If you have, on the evidence or on the law, the doubt of a reasoning and reasonable mind, an intelligent misgiving, then, Sir, I implore you, in

view of the cruel character of this law, in view of
the dreadful consequences of a mistake, send him
not away with that tremendous doubt on your
mind. It may turn to a torturing certainty. The
eyes of many millions are upon you, Sir. You are
to do an act which will hold its place in the history
of America, in the history of the progress of the
human race. May your judgment be for liberty
and not for slavery; for happiness and not for
wretchedness; for hope and not for despair: and
may the blessing of him that is ready to perish
come upon you."

Seth J. Thomas closed the case for the claimant.
After a congratulatory exordium, confessedly in
imitation of Mr. Dana's, he proceeded as follows:

" The claimant in this case, Charles F. Suttle,
says he is of Alexandria, in the state of Virginia;
that, under the laws of that state, he held to service and labor one Anthony Burns, a colored man;
that, on or about the twenty-fourth day of March
last, while so held to service by him, the said
Anthony escaped from the said state of Virginia,
and that he is now here in court. He prays you
(the Commissioner) to hear and consider his proofs
in support of this his claim, and, if they satisfactorily support it, that you will certify to him, under
your hand and seal, that he has a right to transport
him back to Virginia. This is his whole case;
this is all that he asks you to do. Under your certificate, he may take him back to the place from
whence he fled; and he can in virtue of that take
him no where else.

" Now, to entitle the claimant to this certificate, what must he prove? Two things. First, that Burns owed service and labor to him, the claimant. Second, that he escaped. How is he to prove these? The statute answers. He may apply to any court of record in Virginia, or judge thereof in vacation, and make satisfactory proof to such court or judge that Burns owes service or labor to him, and that he escaped. The court shall then cause a record to be made of the matter so proved, and also a general description of the person, with such convenient certainty as may be; and a transcript of such record, authenticated by the attestation of the seal of the court, being produced here where the person is found, and being exhibited to you, is to be taken by you as conclusive of the facts of escape and of service due. And upon the production by the claimant of other and further evidence, if necessary, in respect to the identity of the person escaping, he is to be delivered up to the claimant, with a certificate of his right to take him back; or his claim may be heard upon other satisfactory proofs competent in law.

" Such are the requirements. How have we met them? We have put in the transcript of a record. It is duly authenticated, and is conclusive upon the court of the two facts therein recited, viz., that the claimant held one Anthony Burns to service or labor, and that he escaped. These two facts are not open here. Then the question remains, is the person at the bar, Anthony Burns,

10

as he is called,—nobody thinks of calling him anything else,—is he the Anthony Burns named in the
record? If he is, there is an end of the case.
The claim is made out and the certificate must
follow. This, with simple proof of identity, would
have been all that, in an ordinary case, counsel
would have deemed it necessary to do."

But this was an extraordinary case; and Mr.
Thomas proceeded to say that, in addition to the
record and proof of identity, he had deemed it
proper to put in the testimony of Brent, and the
admissions of Burns. As to the question of identity, there was the description in the record. This
had been objected to by the opposing counsel as
being loose, general in its terms, and defective in
important particulars. Mr. Thomas contended that
it was sufficiently exact to warrant its exclusive
application to the prisoner.

He next considered the array of testimony presented by the defence to prove that Burns was in
Massachusetts during the whole month of March,
and that consequently Brent's story could not be
true. The leading witness was Jones, the colored
man. His testimony was disposed of by the attorney's simple declaration that it was "a story man-
ufactured for the case." But there were seven
other witnesses who had corroborated that "story."
These were disposed of in an equally summary
manner. "Jones," said the claimant's counsel,
"went to them and asked them if they did not
remember the man he had with him cleaning the

windows [at the Mattapan Works], told them this was the man, impressed them with this fact. They came into court with this impression, and made up their minds that he was."

Having thus insisted that the unimpeached testimony for the defence was based upon combined falsehood and delusion, he proceeded by implication to admit its truth. Its force was too great, apparently, even for himself. " Brent," said he, " may possibly be mistaken as to the date." But, the date was not material after all. " A crime of a high nature even may be charged to have been done on the twenty-fourth of March, and proved to have been done on the twenty-fourth of February." Brent could not be mistaken as to the identity. But there was something stronger still — the prisoner's own admissions. Even if it were possible for Brent to be mistaken on the point of identity, such a mistake on the prisoner's part was not possible, and he had admitted that he was Suttle's slave.

The counsel for the defence had contended that, if Anthony owed service at all, it was not to Suttle but to Millspaugh. " If he is the man described," said Mr. Thomas, " that is not open to inquiry. It had been said that under the Commissioner's certificate Anthony might be carried, not to Virginia, but to Cuba or Brazil. They do not tell us how," replied Mr. Thomas. " If he is carried to Cuba, it will not be by your certificate." It had been said that the certificate would send him into

eternal bondage. " It is enough to say," replied
Mr. Thomas, " that it will send him to Virginia
whence he came. When he gets there, he will
have the same rights that he had before he came
here. If that State don't sufficiently guard his
rights, the fault is not yours nor mine." It had
been said that the fugitive slave law was unconstitutional. But, replied Mr. Thomas, it has been
held to be constitutional by the Supreme Court of
Massachusetts, and by every judge before whom a
case under it has arisen.

" It remains only," said Mr. Thomas, " that I
recapitulate the points already stated. The record
is conclusive of two facts, that the person owed
service, and that he escaped. That record, with
the testimony of Brent and the admissions of
Burns, proves the identity. I take leave of the
case, confident in the proofs presented, confident in
the majesty of the law, and confident that the determination here will be just."

At.the conclusion of Mr. Thomas's argument,
the court was adjourned until Friday morning, the
second of June.

CHAPTER VII.

THE DECISION.

DURING Thursday, June first, the popular excitement visibly abated. The unexpected testimony in behalf of Burns had produced a general persuasion that the Commissioner's decision would be made in his favor, and the bare anticipation of this had contributed not a little to compose the public mind. A single incident, however, pointed with ominous certainty to a different result. Early on Friday morning, Burns was presented with a complete new suit of clothes by Butman and the others who had assisted at his capture. A foreknowledge of his impending fate had betrayed them into an act of generosity which would never have been performed, had they believed that he would be suffered to remain on the soil where he had been honestly earning as much, probably, as any of themselves. They imitated the ancient priests by adorning the victim whom they were about to sacrifice.

Arrayed in this holiday garb, Burns was conducted for the last time into the United States court-room. Since Wednesday night, a double guard had been placed over him, and they now at-

10*   (113)

tended him to the dock. Increased precautionary
measures besides had been provided by the Marshal. Soldiers with fixed bayonets filled all the
avenues, and bullies armed with bludgeons and
pistols crowded the court-room. One at a time,
members of the bar, reporters for the press, friends
of the prisoner, and favored citizens, defiled beneath
crossed bayonets and occupied their places.

At nine o'clock, Commissioner Loring took his
seat upon the bench. His countenance wore a
haggard and jaded aspect, his port and bearing
were not those of a judge clear in his great office.
Hardly glancing at the assembly before him, amidst
profound stillness he immediately began to read
his decision. It was in the following words:

THE DECISION.

" The issue between the parties arises under the
United States statute of 1850, and for the respondent it is urged that the statute is unconstitutional.
Whenever this objection is made, it becomes necessary to recur to the purpose of the statute. It
purports to carry into execution the provision of
the Constitution, which provides for the extradition
of persons held to service or labor in one state,
and escaping to another. It is applicable, and it
is applied alike to bond and free, to the apprentice
and the slave; and in reference to both, its purpose,
provisions, and processes are the same.

" The arrest of the fugitive is a ministerial and
not a judicial act, and the nature of the act is not

altered by the means employed for its accomplishment. When an officer arrests a fugitive from justice, or a party accused, the officer must determine the identity, and use his discretion and information for the purpose. When an arrest is made under this statute, the means of determining the identity are prescribed by the statute; but when the means are used and the act is done, it is still a ministerial act. The statute only substitutes the means it provides, for the discretion of an arresting officer, and thus gives to the fugitive from service a much better protection than a fugitive from justice can claim under any law.

" If extradition is the only purpose of the statute, and the determination of the identity is the only purpose of these proceedings under it, it seems to me that the objection of unconstitutionality to the statute, because it does not furnish a jury trial to the fugitive, is answered; there is no provision in the Constitution requiring that the *identity* of the person to be arrested should be determined by a jury. It has never been claimed for apprentices or fugitives from justice, and if it does not belong to them, it does not belong to the respondent.

" And if extradition is a ministerial act, to substitute, in its performance, for the discretion of an arresting officer, the discretion of a Commissioner instructed by testimony under oath, seems scarcely to reach to a grant of judicial power, within the meaning of the United States Constitution. And it is certain that if the power given to, and used by, the Commissioner of United States Courts under the statute is unconstitutional, then so was the power given to, and used by, magistrates of counties, cities and towns, and used by the act of 1793. These all were Commissioners of the United States; the powers they used under the statute, were not derived from the laws of their respective states, but from the statute of the United States. They were commissioned by that, and that alone. They were commissioned by the class instead of individually and by name, and in this respect the only difference that I can see between the acts of 1793 and 1850, is, that the latter reduced the number of appointees, and confined the appointment to those who, by their professional standing, should be competent to the performance of their duties, and who bring to them the certificates of the highest judicial tribunals of the land.

" It is said the statute is unconstitutional, because it gives to the record of the court of Virginia an effect beyond its constitutional effect. The first section of the fourth article of the Constitution is directory only on the State power, and as to the State courts, and does not seek to limit the control of Congress over the tribunals of the United States or the proceedings therein. Then in that article the term, 'records and judicial proceedings,' refers to such *inter pártes*, and of necessity can have no application to proceedings avowedly *ex parte*. Then if the first section includes this record, it expressly declares as to 'records and judicial proceedings' that Congress shall prescribe '*the effect thereof*,' and this express power would seem to be precisely the power that Congress has used in the statute of 1850.

" Other constitutional objections have been urged here, which have been adjudged and re-adjudged by the Courts of the United States, and of many of the states; and the decisions of these tribunals absolve me from considering the same questions further than to apply to them the determination of the Supreme Court of this state in Sims' case, 7 Cushing 309, that they 'are settled by a course of legal decisions which we are bound to respect, and which we regard as binding and conclusive on this Court.'

" But a special objection has been raised to the record that it describes the escape as *from* the State of Virginia, and omits to describe it as *into another State*, in the words and substance of the Constitution. But in this the record follows the tenth section of the statute of 1850, and the context of the section confines its action to cases of escape from one state, &c., into another, and is therefore in practical action and extent strictly conformable to the Constitution.

" This statute has been decided to be constitutional by the unanimous opinion of the Judges of the Supreme Court of Massachusetts on the fullest argument and maturest deliberation, and to be the law of Massachusetts, as well as, and because it is a constitutional law of the United States; and the wise words of our revered Chief Justice in that case, 7 Cushing, 318, may well be repeated now, and remembered always. The Chief Justice says:

" 'Slavery was not created, established, or perpetuated, by the Constitution; it existed before; it would have existed if the Constitution had not been made. The framers of the Constitution could not abrogate slavery, or the rights claimed under it. They took it as they found it, and regulated it to a limited extent. The Constitution, therefore, is not responsible for the origin or continuance of slavery; the provision it contains was the best adjustment which could be made of conflicting rights and claims, and was absolutely necessary to effect what may now be considered as the general pacification, by which harmony and peace should take the place of violence and war. These were the circumstances, and this the spirit, in which the Constitution was made; the regulation of slavery, so far as to prohibit States by law from harboring fugitive slaves, was an essential element in its formation, and the Union intended to be established by it was essentially necessary to the peace, happiness, and highest prosperity of all the States. In this spirit, and with these views steadily in prospect, it seems to be the duty of all judges and magistrates to expound and apply these provisions in the Constitution and laws of the United States, and in this spirit it behoves all persons bound to obey the laws of the United States, to consider and regard them.'

" It is said that the statute, if constitutional, is wicked and cruel. The like charges were brought against the act of 1793; and Chief Justice Parker, of Massachusetts, made the answer which Chief Justice Shaw cites and approves, viz : — ' Whether the statute is a harsh one or not, it is not for us to determine.'

" It is said that the statute is so cruel and wicked that it should not be executed by good men. Then into what hands shall its administration fall, and in its administration, what is to be the protection of the unfortunate men who are brought within its operation? Will those who call the statute merciless, commit it to a merciless judge?

" If the statute involves that right, which for us makes life sweet, and the want of which makes life a misfortune, shall its administration be confined to those who are reckless of that right to others, or ignorant or careless of the means given for its legal defence, or dishonest in their use? If any men wish this, they are more cruel and wicked than the statute, for they would strip from the fugitive the best security and every alleviation the statute leaves him.[1]

---

[1] The reasoning in these two paragraphs presents one of the most remarkable instances of moral obliquity on record. The assertion is, that a certain statute is so wicked that good men ought not to execute it. Judge Loring, on the other hand, says that good men are the very persons to execute it. Of course they are so to execute it as either to promote or to defeat its true intent. Judge Loring will certainly say that they should execute it after the former method. That is, good men are to engage deliberately, and under oath, in promoting a wicked design !

" I think the statute constitutional, and it remains for me now to apply it to the facts of the
case. The facts to be proved by the claimant are
three :

" First, That Anthony Burns owed him service
in Virginia. Second, That Anthony Burns escaped from that service. These facts he has proved
by the record which the statute, section tenth,
declares ' shall be held and taken to be full and *conclusive* evidence of the fact of escape, and that the
service or labor of the person escaping is due to the
party in such record mentioned.' Thus these two
facts are removed entirely and absolutely from my
jurisdiction, and I am entirely and absolutely precluded from applying evidence to them. If, therefore, there is in the case evidence capable of such
application, I cannot make it.

" The third fact is, the identity of the party
before me with the Anthony Burns mentioned in
the record.

" This identity is the only question I have a
right to consider. To this, and to this alone, I am
to apply the evidence ; and the question whether
the respondent was in Virginia or Massachusetts
at a certain time, is material only as it is evidence
on the point of identity. So the parties have used
it, and the testimony of the complainant being that
the Anthony Burns of the record was in Virginia
on the nineteenth of March last, the evidence of
the respondent has been offered to show that he
was in Massachusetts on or about the first of
March last, and thereafter till now.

" The testimony of the claimant is from a single witness, and he standing in circumstances that would necessarily bias the fairest mind; but other imputation than this has not been offered against him, and, from anything that has appeared before me, cannot be. His means of knowledge are personal, direct, and qualify him to testify confidently, and he has done so.

" The testimony on the part of the respondent is from many witnesses whose integrity is admitted, and to whom no imputation of bias can be attached by the evidence in the case, and whose means of knowledge are personal and direct, but in my opinion less full and complete than that of Mr. Brent.

" Then, between the testimony of the claimant and respondent there is a conflict, complete and irreconcilable. The question of identity on such a conflict of testimony is not unprecedented nor uncommon in judicial proceedings, and the trial of Dr. Webster furnished a memorable instance of it.

" The question now is, whether there is other evidence in this case which will determine this conflict. In every case of disputed identity there is one person, always, whose knowledge is perfect and positive, and whose evidence is not within the reach of error; and that is the person whose identity is questioned, and such evidence this case affords. The evidence is of the conversation which took place between Burns and the claimant on the night of the arrest.

11

" When the claimant entered the room where Burns was, Burns saluted him, and by his *Christian* name : — ' How do you do, Master *Charles?* ' He saluted Mr. Brent also, and by his *Christian* name: — ' How do you do, Master *William?* ' (To the appellation ' Master ' I give no weight.)

" Colonel Suttle said, — ' How came you here? ' Burns said an accident had happened to him ; that he was working down at Roberts', on board a vessel, got tired and went to sleep, and was carried off in the vessel. ' Anthony, did I ever whip you?' — ' No, sir.' — ' Did I ever hire you out where you did not wish to go? ' — ' No, sir.' — ' Have you ever asked me for money when I did not give it to you?' — ' No, sir.' — ' When you were sick, did I not prepare you a bed in my own house and put you upon it and nurse you?' — ' Yes, sir.' Something was said about going back. He was asked if he was willing to go back, and he said, ' Yes, he was.'

" This was the testimony of Mr. Brent. That a conversation took place, was confirmed by the testimony of Caleb Page, who was present, and added the remark, that Burns said he did not come in Capt. Snow's vessel. The cross-examination of Brent showed that Col. Suttle said, ' I make you no promises and I make you no threats.'

" To me this evidence, when applied to the question of identity, confirms and establishes the testimony of Mr. Brent in its conflict with that offered on the part of the respondent ; and then, on the whole testimony, my mind is satisfied beyond a reasonable doubt of the identity of the respondent with the Anthony Burns named in the record.

" It was objected that this conversation was in the nature of admissions, and that too of a man stupefied by circumstances and fear, and these considerations would have weight had the admissions been used to establish the truth of the matters to which they referred, i. e., the usage, the giving of money, nursing, &c.; but they were used for no such purpose, but only as evidence in reference to identity. Had they been procured by hope or fear they would have been inadmissible; but of that I considered there was no evidence.

" On the law and facts of the case, I consider the claimant entitled to the certificate from me which he claims." [1]

The Commissioner folded his manuscript and prepared to take his departure. But the auditors remained in their places, and for some moments the dead silence continued unbroken. Then, as at a funeral, one and another went quietly to Burns, whispered a word of sympathy, and bade him farewell; and gradually, the court-room was vacated by all but the Marshal, his aids, and the prisoner.

[1] Shortly after the rendition of Burns, an article was published in the Boston Atlas, entitled, "The Decision which Judge Loring might have given." It has since been acknowledged by Richard H. Dana, Jr., to be his production. The reader will find it worth while to compare it with Judge Loring's actual decision. See Appendix D

CHAPTER VIII.

THE SURRENDER.

BEFORE ten o'clock the decision had been pronounced. The act of rendition alone remained to be accomplished. It was the most momentous part of the whole transaction. In a community proverbially devoted to law and order, it had become perilous to attempt the execution of such a judicial sentence. The fact that a similar sentence had once before been executed in the same community, so far from making a repetition of the act more easy, only made it more difficult. But the difficulties had been immeasurably increased by the passage of the Nebraska Bill. All through the winter and spring, the people of Massachusetts had been kept at fever heat by the debates in Congress upon that daring and Union-shattering measure. While the trial of Burns was going on, came the news of its passage through both Houses. On the day before his extradition, the telegraph announced that the bill had received the President's signature, and had become the supreme law of the land. At such a juncture, the thrice and four times odious fugitive slave law had demanded another victim. It seemed like adding insult to injury. At the moment, many regarded the arrest of Burns as a thing arranged by the Federal Government for the express purpose of showing to the country that not even the passage of the Nebraska Bill would prevent the execution of the slave law.

Excited by this state of things, the people had thronged to the trial of Burns in an unexampled manner. They came, not from Boston only, nor from suburban towns only, but from distant cities and villages of Massachusetts.[1] Day after day, during the week of the trial, the Square around the Court House had been filled by the throng; but on the last day, and when it became known that the prisoner was to be sent back, the mass of spectators was swollen to such an extent that the previous multitude seemed as nothing in comparison. Of this countless number, an overwhelming majority were bitterly hostile to the execution of the law; many had sworn that it should not be executed on that day. In the face of such a formidable popular demonstration, it now became the duty of the federal officers to remove the prisoner, a third of a mile, from the Court House to the vessel lying at the wharf.

There were two distinct objects to be accomplished,—the removal of the prisoner, and the pre-

---

[1] Six or seven hundred went down in a body from the city of Worcester, distant forty-four miles from Boston. Many of them were men from the machine-shops and factories, whom no ordinary motive would have led to forsake their business.

11*

servation of the peace of the city. The charge of
the former devolved upon the United States Marshal, that of the latter upon the Mayor of Boston.
But there was danger of confounding the two objects; special care was needed to provide that,
under the guise of protecting the city, the Mayor's
force should not be implicated in the act of rendition. The crisis called for a magistrate who fully
understood the limits of his official duty and possessed firmness enough to maintain his position.
Unfortunately, the Mayor's chair was at this time
occupied by one whose qualifications, natural and
acquired, but ill prepared him to cope with the difficulties of his situation. Bred a physician, and
transferred at once from the routine of a prac-
titioner to the chief magistracy of the city, Mayor
Smith had neither that intimate knowledge of his
legal responsibilities which the crisis demanded,
nor that firmness of character which would enable
him to maintain a consistent course. In the outset, he had committed himself to the Faneuil Hall
meeting. When the time for holding that meeting
arrived, he excused himself from personally attending it, but authorized assurances to be given of his
hearty sympathy. When consulted by his policemen, on the morning after the riot, he informed
them that they were to render no aid to the Marshal in the rendition of Burns. Beginning thus on
the side of the people, he yet ended by involving
himself, the police of Boston, and the military of

the Commonwealth, in the task of carrying into execution the fugitive slave act.

The arrangements were concerted and dictated by Benjamin F. Hallett, Watson Freeman, and Benjamin F. Edmands. Mr. Hallett, the leading spirit of the trio, was a politician in whom a strong desire for popularity among the masses, was constantly overmastered by a stronger desire for the patronage of the Federal Government. Accordingly, while he had made an occasional venture to secure the former, his heartiest and most persevering activity was expended in pursuit of the latter.[1] As the reward of his devotion, not to say servility, the Government had benefieed him with the office of United States Attorney for the District of Massachusetts. This position, he seemed to imagine, gave him the right on the present occasion to direct the conduct, not only of other officers of the Federal Government, but also of the officers of the Commonwealth. Mr. Freeman, the Marshal, was a person in whom animal courage, decision, and resoluteness of purpose, were marked

[1] At an earlier period of his life, Mr. Hallett was, for three or four years, associated with William Lloyd Garrison in the promulgation of the latter's anti-slavery views, and was as much entitled to be called a Garrisonian as any other person of that party. He assembled with them, had a conspicuous place on their platform, made speeches for them, reported their doings (being a stenographer), and in other ways signalized his zeal in the cause. Viewing him in that stage of his development by the reflected light of his after career, one must have been tempted to exclaim, " Is Saul also among the prophets ? "

characteristics. Upon him devolved the sole responsibility of every step taken in the executive
act of rendition. But he naturally deferred to the
law officer of the Government, and his name was
used to give sanction to the plans of the Attorney.
Mr. Edmands was a major-general, commanding
the first division of the Massachusetts Volunteer
Militia. Leading the useful but inglorious life of
a druggist in State Street for the most part of the
time, he enjoyed the distinction of going into
camp once a year, and there receiving the homage
of his troops. But holiday shows of soldiery are
apt to pall, and Mr. Edmands, not improbably,
was ready to make the most of an occasion that
promised him the novel experience of being engaged in real service. Whatever his motive, it led
him into the grave indecorum of stepping out of
his subordinate position as a military officer, and
assuming the character of dictator to his civil
superior.

Having decided upon the course to be pursued,
these persons threw themselves upon the Mayor,
for the purpose of coercing him into the adoption
of their measures. They commenced their efforts
for this end at an early stage of the trial. They
sought and obtained personal interviews with him
at the City Hall. They addressed to him repeated
letters of remonstrance and advice. The result
was, that the Mayor abandoned his first purpose,
surrendered his own judgment, and conformed his
official conduct to the programme which they had

marked out. The correspondence which passed between the several parties clearly developed this change, and the influences by which it was effected.

From the night of the riot until the Tuesday following, two companies of the city soldiery had been under arms for the preservation of the peace. On that day, the Marshal and the Attorney addressed a formal communication to the Mayor, declaring that force to be insufficient for the purpose, and expressing the opinion that the entire command of Gen. Edmands within the city would be requisite. The Mayor's view of the case was the reverse of this.

" After a full examination of the condition of the city this morning," said he, in a note to Gen. Edmands, dated May 31st, "I feel justified in saying that one military company will be amply sufficient, from this date till further orders, to maintain order and suppress any riotous proceedings."

He therefore directed Gen. Edmands to discharge one of the two companies at nine o'clock on that morning. This order was followed by another, bearing the same date, and directed to the same officer, in which, after declaring that it had been made to appear to him that a mob was threatened, the Mayor commanded Gen. Edmands to cause an entire Brigade, together with an additional corps of Cadets, to be paraded on the morning of June second, for the purpose of repressing the anticipated tumult.[1]   This sudden and extraordinary change of opinion and conduct was caused by no popular outbreak unexpectedly arising after the first order for discharging the company had been issued.   The cause was suggested by Mayor Smith himself in his answers to certain interrogatories subsequently made under oath.[2]   " Mr. Hallett and Mr. Freeman called upon me," said he, "some two or three days before the second of June, and expressed an opinion that the military force then on duty was inadequate to the maintenance of the peace of the city.   I was soon convinced that more force was necessary, and at once took measures accordingly."   In addition to this personal interview, the Marshal and Attorney addressed to him, under date of May 31st, a joint communication in which the same views were urged upon his consideration.[3]   The interview and the despatch of the letter manifestly occurred in the interval between the issuing of the Mayor's two contradictory orders of that day.   It thus appeared that while the Mayor's own careful observation of the condi-

[1] See Appendix F.

[2] In the case of Ela *vs.* Smith and others, growing out of the assault of the soldiers upon the plaintiff.

[3] A curious proof of the District Attorney's usurping disposition was disclosed by the communications which were addressed to the Mayor, by the Marshal and himself.   The first was signed by the Marshal alone, and was simply endorsed " approved " by Mr. Hallett.   The second was signed by both ; but the name of the Marshal, who was the chief and only really responsible officer, was placed beneath that of the Attorney.   See Appendix G.

tion of the city had convinced him that but one
company of military was necessary, the representations of the United States officers convinced him,
an hour or two after, that a whole Brigade was
necessary.

The ostensible object of the extraordinary inter-
ference by the United States officers with the
Mayor's functions, was the preservation of the
peace of the city. " The Marshal does not ask
any aid to execute the fugitive law as such," said
that officer in his communication of May 30th;
"nothing is required but the preservation of the
peace of the city." " We repeat what we have
before said, that the United States officers do not
desire you to execute the process under the fugitive law of the United States, which devolves on
them alone in the discharge of their duties; but
they call upon you as the conservator of the peace
of the city ; " — so wrote both the District Attorney and the Marshal in their communication of
May 31st. " They distinctly and explicitly declare that the United States Government neither
wished nor asked any assistance from the city of
Boston ; " — so said the Mayor in his sworn answers at a subsequent date.

Unfortunately for this pretence, the same correspondence showed that the design was to enlist the
troops of Massachusetts, in effect, though not in
form, in the service of the United States. In their
first communication, the two functionaries of the

Federal Government, while disclaiming any authority, declared their belief that the expenses incurred by mustering the large military force which they called on the Mayor for, would be met by the President. The Mayor hesitated; their "belief" was not a sufficient guarantee. He addressed to them a note of inquiry touching that point. In the interval, Mr. Hallett, still taking the lead in another man's business, had sought and obtained from the President full authority for incurring the proposed expense.[1]   In the next communication, accordingly, the assurance of this authority, confirmed by a copy of the President's despatch, was given to the Mayor. Then immediately followed the order for mustering the Brigade. It seemed clear, therefore, on the one hand, that if, in the Mayor's judgment, there had been a real necessity for calling out a Brigade to preserve the peace of Boston, he would not have waited for an assurance that the expense would be met by a foreign government; and on the other hand, that the President would not have felt authorized to draw money from the national treasury for the purpose of preserving the peace of a municipal corpora-

---

[1] Throughout the whole affair, a frequent correspondence by telegraph was kept up between the United States officers at Boston and the President at Washington. The zeal and vigor which the Federal Executive displayed in enforcing an odious statute on this occasion, stands in striking contrast to his indifference, not to say connivance, on a later occasion, at the most high-handed violation of the Constitution and the laws. See Appendix H.

tion.[1] The tenor of his note to Mr. Hallett, singularly at variance with the latter's pretences, placed the matter beyond a doubt. "Incur," said he, "any expense deemed necessary by the Marshal and yourself for city military or otherwise, *to insure the execution of the law.*" Yielding to a requisition based upon such a document, the Mayor did, in effect, constitute the Massachusetts troops a part of the Marshal's armed posse comitatus.

The order for mustering the Brigade, which was signed by the Mayor and directed to Gen. Edmands, was drawn up by the latter officer. Distrusting his superior's knowledge of the military statutes, and confident of his own, he had assumed the task of preparing the formula that was to govern his own action. A police captain, upon entering the City Hall on the morning of June first, met Gen. Edmands descending from the Mayor's private room. As they entered the Police Office together, the military chief displayed the order with the Mayor's signature fresh upon it. "There,"

[1] The sum of fourteen thousand dollars, or thereabouts, was paid out of the United States treasury to Mayor Smith, for services rendered on this occasion by the Massachusetts militia. This money was paid by him directly to the several companies, without passing into the city treasury or in any way coming under the control of the city government. No record exists at the City Hall that any such transaction ever took place. In disbursing the money, therefore, Dr. Smith acted, not in his capacity as Mayor, or as magistrate, but as an agent of the Federal Government. He supported two distinct characters in the tragedy — that of a Massachusetts magistrate in calling out the troops, and that of a Federal disbursing agent in paying them.

said he, "is the only order ever yet drawn up under which the military could legally act;" and, with some disparaging remarks on the ignorance of civilians in such matters, he proceeded to claim it as the triumph of his own genius. Then, as if for the purpose of justifying such a formidable military demonstration as that which the order contemplated, he turned and demanded of the police captain what those men were hid away for in Tremont Temple. " There are a thousand armed men there," said he. The policeman doubted the extraordinary statement. " Yes, there are," reiterated the general in a heat; " a gentleman who saw them told me; d—n them," continued he, with a profane zeal worthy of his cause, "we 'll fix 'em." The thousand men were " men in buckram."

Armed with the authority conveyed by this precept, Gen. Edmands proceeded to issue his orders for assembling the troops. At half-past eight o'clock on the morning of June second, the whole force paraded on Boston Common. It consisted of the First Battalion of Light Dragoons, the Fifth Regiment of Artillery, the Fifth Regiment of Light Infantry, the Third Battalion of Light Infantry, and the corps of Cadets. In all, there were twenty-two companies, including two of cavalry, and not less than a thousand soldiers. These troops were as fine specimens of the citizen soldiery of the Union as could anywhere be found. Often had they, on parade days, attracted the admiration of their fellow-citizens by their martial bearing, the tasteful splendor of their uniforms, and the perfection of their drill. As the product of free institutions, they were held in just pride by the whole community, and never had an occasion arisen to interrupt the sympathy between the two classes. Now, for the first time, were these troops drawn up in hostile array against the people, to assist in executing the most odious statute that ever found a place in the archives of a free republic. The spectacle turned the popular complacency in their favorites into indignation and disgust.

A strong *esprit du corps*, together with the military maxim of unquestioning obedience, sufficed to bring out the companies with full ranks. But they were far from being unanimous in their approval of the object for which they were called forth. A keen sense of the ignominy to which they were subjected, filled the breasts of some, and caused them to hang their heads with shame. Some were indifferent to the moral character of the occasion, but were anxious to signalize their soldiership. Others sympathized with the slave-hunter and rejoiced in the opportunity to render him aid with ball and bayonet. The general habits and conduct of these latter corresponded with their disposition. As they stood in line on the Common, they compromised the character of the whole corps by their free use of intoxicating liquor and the singing of ribald songs. At a later period in the day, a company or detachment posted in State street, opposite the Exchange, quite bore off the palm of infamy by conduct of this sort. Filled with liquor, even to intoxication, they became lost to all sense of decorum, and, reeling upon their gunstocks, sang the chorus, " Oh, carry me back to Old Virginny."

The character and conduct of the officers were as diverse as those of the men. Some went to the discharge of their duty, cursing the authorities who had imposed it upon them. Some pressed forward with alacrity as to congenial business. Conspicuous among the subalterns, was the commander of the Light Dragoons. His intemperate zeal for the maintenance of law on this occasion, was in striking contrast with the disposition which he manifested at a later period, when, at a convivial entertainment of the soldiery, he bade open defiance to a recently enacted statute that was intended to deprive him, and such as him, of their favorite beverages. The day did not pass without his giving in his own person a humiliating proof of the necessity of such a law. While endeavoring to ride down a nimble bystander whose sole offence was the expression of an opinion, he reeled from his saddle and fell prostrate upon the pavement.

The part to be performed by the police in the act of rendition, as well as that of the military, was prescribed by the United States officers. On the morning of Friday, June second, the Chief of the Police summoned his deputy and the captains of the several stations into his office, and locked the door. He then produced a diagram of Court

Square, Court and State streets, and of the streets and avenues leading into them, together with certain written instructions, all of which he had received from the Mayor.[1] The diagram, he informed his subordinates, represented the section of the city which was to be entirely cleared of the people and to be taken possession of by the military and police. He then proceeded to impart to the assembled captains their instructions. Among the number was Joseph K. Hayes, captain of the South Station. This officer had already acted a significant part in the business. On the morning after the attack on the Court House, he had called at the Chief's office for orders; he was directed to bring up fifteen of his men and station them in the office of the Water Registrar, opening upon the Square. Having obeyed the order, he forthwith sought the Mayor, and inquired what his men were to do.

" Are we to help the slave-catchers ? " said he.

" No," replied the Mayor, " protect the property and lives of the citizens — nothing more."

Captain Hayes returned to his men and informed them of his interview with the Mayor, and of the instructions which he had received.

" Now," continued he, " I wish you distinctly to understand how much I shall help the United States in this business. If there is an attempt at a rescue, and it is likely to fail, I shall help the rescuers." In accordance with his expectation and

[1] See Appendix I.

12*

wish, this speech was immediately reported to the Chief by some of the men under his command.

Mr. Hayes was the first to receive his instructions. He was directed to take his men, pass down State street, and notify each occupant of the buildings on the right, that by the Mayor's command they were to close their places of business. Having reached Commercial street, he was to draw up his men in a line across that street, cause them to join hands, and in that manner force back the crowd to Milk street, where he was to hold them at all hazards. Immediately after, a detachment of military was to be posted across Commercial, at its junction with State street. The whole space in Commercial street, between Milk and State streets, would thus be kept vacant. He was further instructed that, if his police force should be unable to maintain their stand against the pressure of the crowd, they were to swing back right and left; *this was to be a signal to the military at the other end, who had instructions instantly, without giving warning, to fire upon the crowd.*

The same instructions were repeated to the rest of the captains. Each was charged with the duty of clearing a particular street, each was to be followed by a military detachment, having orders to fire without warning.

Mr. Hayes listened attentively to this programme. " Mr. Chief," said he, " does not this look like helping to carry off Burns?" The Chief, with some embarrassment, made an indistinct reply. Just then a tap was made on the door. Upon its being opened, the Mayor entered, and bowing to those present said :

" The Commissioner has just entered the court-room to give his decision, and has required me to see that the Square and the various avenues are cleared." Then, instructing the Chief forthwith to attend to that duty, he withdrew. Mr. Hayes again spoke :

" The Commissioner gives directions to the Mayor, the Mayor to the Chief of Police, the Chief to his captains, they to their men ; this is a pretty strong chain binding us to the act of rendition."

Without further words, he retired to another room, wrote a resignation of his office, and then, entering the Mayor's private apartment, placed it in his hands. Greatly agitated, the Mayor entreated him to revoke it, but Mr. Hayes had not acted hastily, and remained immovable. Taking a copy of his resignation, he carried it to the office of one of the newspaper presses, which, during this memorable occasion, were throwing off editions at all hours of the day, and within an hour's time it was scattered over the whole city.[1]

The resignation of Mr. Hayes seriously deranged the plans of the Mayor and his advisers. They had intended to disguise the employment of the military by pushing the police prominently forward.

[1] This act, so rare in the history of official life, involved the sacrifice, not only of assured position, but also of the most flattering prospects. But it had its reward. See Appendix J.

The police were to clear the streets, they only were
to come in contact with the people and force them
back beyond the outer barrier of the reserved section.   When this was complete and the space
clear, the military were to march in and take up
the several positions assigned them.   The failure
of the police to accomplish their part of the task
made it necessary to call in the aid of the military.
The selection of the officer to whom the business
was entrusted, was significant of the influences
that controlled the proceedings.   This was Isaac H.
Wright.   He was one of the very few men of Massachusetts who had set at naught the principles of
their fathers by volunteering in the war with Mexico.   The fellow-officer of Gen. Pierce in that
wicked raid, his equal in military skill, not less his
equal in moral character, scarcely his inferior as a
claimant upon his party for promotion, of congenial
habits, and like him often hazarding all upon a powerful flow of spirits, he was yet, unlike him, made to
feel full sorely the caprice of Democracy in the distri-
bution of political favors.   For while Gen. Pierce,
returning from the plains of Mexico, had been
wafted into the Presidential Chair by prosperous
winds blowing from all quarters, Col. Wright was
left to exchange the sword for the hammer and to
settle down into the humdrum life of an auctioneer.
He was now, however, the captain of the Light
Dragoons, and no officer in all the Massachusetts
troops was more ready to assist in the execution
of the fugitive slave act than himself.   In commit-

ting to him and his mounted Dragoons the duty of driving the citizens from their thoroughfares and places of business, the authorities could not expect that any tenderness would temper their zeal.

In the midst of these preparations, the city was electrified by the following proclamation which was posted at the corners of the streets:

TO THE CITIZENS OF BOSTON.[1]

To secure order throughout the city this day, Major-General Edmands and the Chief of Police will make such disposition of the respective forces under their commands as will best promote that important object; and they are clothed with full discretionary power to sustain the laws of the land. All well-disposed citizens and other persons are urgently requested to leave those streets which it may be found necessary to clear temporarily, and under no circumstances to obstruct or molest any officer, civil or military, in the lawful discharge of his duty.   J. V. C. SMITH, *Mayor*.

BOSTON, June 2, 1854.

By this proclamation the whole city was in effect placed under martial law. It notified the citizens that the Mayor had, for the time, delegated his power to a military officer and abdicated his office. The legality of this step was afterward seriously called in question. Among others who took this

---

[1] This proclamation was printed before the Commissioner's decision had been pronounced.

ground, was Peleg W. Chandler, then a member of the Executive Council of the Commonwealth, and previously, Solicitor for the city of Boston.   In an argument that never was refuted, he examined the Mayor's whole course in relation to the military, and maintained that in several particulars he had acted without warrant of law.[1]

About eleven o'clock, the troops on the Common received orders to move down into Court and State streets.   Each man had been supplied with eleven rounds of powder and ball, and, before moving, they proceeded to load in the presence of the assembled spectators.   Then, without music, they marched down through the above-named streets, dropping off detachments at the several side streets, until the whole were posted.

Meanwhile, the Marshal had been making his own preparations.   One hundred and twenty-five men were sworn in as specials.   Some of these were tide-waiters, truckmen, and other dependents upon the Custom House; all were taken from the least reputable portion of the citizens of Boston. No better could be obtained.   So great had been the change in public opinion since the extradition of Sims, when merchants, bankers, ship-owners, and others of repute had pressed forward with offers of personal service in forcing back that hapless negro into slavery and death.   These specials

---

[1] See Boston Atlas of June 12th and 16th, 1854.   I much regret that the length of this able argument precludes its insertion in this volume.

were assembled in the Court House, and armed with cutlasses, pistols, and billies. They were then placed under the command of one Peter T. Dunbar, a Custom House truckman, who led them into an upper hall of the building, and there drilled them in marching and other exercises before the door of Burns's cell. Besides these, the Marshal had assembled five companies of United States troops, numbering one hundred and forty men; and, to complete his array, a brass cannon had been transported from the Navy Yard in Charlestown, at early dawn, and planted in the Square.

At eleven o'clock, Court Square presented a spectacle that became indelibly engraved upon the memories of men. The people had been swept out of the Square, and stood crowded together in Court street, presenting to the eye a solid rampart of living beings. At the eastern door of the Court House, stood the cannon, loaded, and with its mouth pointed full upon the compact mass. By its side stood the officer commanding the detachment of United States troops, gazing with steady composure in the same direction. It was the first time that the armed power of the United States had ever been arrayed against the people of Massachusetts. Men who witnessed the sight, and reflected upon its cause, were made painfully to recognize the fact, before unfelt, that they were the subjects of two governments.

After the decision, Burns remained in the court-room awaiting the hour of his departure. The retainers of the Marshal crowded around him with attempts at consolation. His guards especially endeavored to cheer his spirits. They gave him four dollars; they assured him that it was their intention to purchase his freedom; they had made arrangements with his owner, they said, and had already obtained four hundred dollars toward the object. To all these professions and promises Burns paid little heed; they came from the same men who had captured him. At length, Deputy Marshal Riley entered the room and ordered him to be handcuffed. Burns earnestly remonstrated against the indignity; he gave assurances that he would pass through the streets quietly, if allowed to go unshackled, otherwise, he threatened to make every demonstration of violence in his power. Butman thereupon left the room, and sought the Marshal's permission to dispense with the instruments of disgrace; and, in spite of counsel to the contrary from some cowardly adviser who stood by, the request was granted. The slavery into which Burns was returning was an evil which he had borne from the cradle, but the iron fetters were symbols of disgrace which his unbroken spirit was not prepared to endure.

One o'clock had arrived, and yet the movement of the *cortege* was delayed. Meanwhile, Gen. Edmands had from time to time dashed into the Square, and, dismounting, held hurried conferences with the Marshal in the building. A bystander who heard their conversation, learned that the delay was caused by the General's inability to clear the streets, and his fear of being unable to accomplish the task he had undertaken.

At length, about two o'clock, the column was formed in the Square. First came a detachment of United States Artillery, followed by a platoon of United States Marines. After these followed the armed civil posse of the Marshal, to which succeeded two platoons of Marines. The cannon, guarded by another platoon of Marines, brought up the rear. When this arrangement was completed, Burns, accompanied by a officer on each side with arms interlocked, was conducted from his prison through a passage lined with soldiers, and placed in the centre of the armed posse. Immediately after the decision, Mr. Dana and Mr. Grimes had asked permission to walk with Burn's arm in arm, from the Court House to the vessel at the wharf; and the Marshal had given them his consent. At the last moment, he sought them out and requested that they would not insist upon the performance of his promise, because, in the opinion of some of the military officers, such a spectacle would add to the excitement. Mr. Dana declined to release the Marshal from his promise. The latter persisted in urging the abandonment of the purpose.

"Do I understand you," asked Mr. Dana, "to say distinctly that we *shall not* accompany Burns, after having given your promise that we might?"

The Marshal winced under the pressure of this

13

pointed question, but after a momentary reluctance answered firmly, " Yes." Accordingly, without a single friend at his side, and hemmed in by a thick-set hedge of gleaming blades, Burns took his departure.

The route from the Court House to the wharf had by this time become thronged with a countless multitude. It seemed as if the whole population of the city had been concentrated upon this narrow space. In vain the military and police had attempted to clear the streets; the carriage-way alone was kept vacant. On the sidewalks in Court and State streets, every available spot was occupied; all the passages, windows, and balconies, from basement to attic, overflowed with gazers, while the roofs of the buildings were black with human beings. It was computed that not less than fifty thousand people had gathered to witness the spectacle.

At different points along the route, were displayed symbols significant of the prevailing senti-ment. A distinguished member of the Suffolk Bar, whose office was directly opposite the court-room, and who was, at the time, commander of the Ancient and Honorable Artillery, draped his windows in mourning. The example was quickly followed by others. From a window opposite the Old State House, was suspended a black coffin, upon which was the legend, *The Funeral of Liberty*. At a point farther on toward the wharf, a venerable merchant had caused a rope to be stretched from his own warehouse across State street to an opposite point, and the American flag, draped in mourning, to be suspended therefrom with the union down. On looking forth from his window some time after, he saw a man intent on casting a cord over the rope, for the purpose of tearing down the flag.

"Rascal!" shouted the old man, as he sallied forth with his long white hair streaming behind, "desist, or I'll prosecute you."

"I am an American," answered the other, "and am not going to see the flag of my country disgraced."

"I too am an American, and a native of this city," retorted the State street merchant, "and I declare that my country is eternally disgraced by this day's proceedings. That flag hangs there by my orders: touch it at your peril." The flag remained, until the transaction of which, in its dishonor, it was a fit emblem, was fully ended.

Along this Via Dolorosa, with its cloud of witnesses, the column now began to move. No music enlivened its march; the dull tramp of the soldiers on the rocky pavements, and the groans and hisses of the bystanders, were the only sounds. As it proceeded, its numbers were swelled by unexpected additions. Unauthorized, the zealous commander of the mounted Dragoons joined it with his corps. The Lancers, jealous of their

rivals, hastened to follow the example: thus van-
guard and rear-guard consisted of Massachusetts
troops. In its progress, it went past the Old State
House, where, in 1646, the founders of the Commonwealth enacted that solemn condemnation of
human slavery, which stands at the beginning of
this volume.[1] Just below, it passed over the
ground where, in the Massacre of 1770, fell
Attucks, the first negro martyr in the cause of
American liberty.

Opposite the Custom House, the column turned
at a right angle into another street. This cross
movement suddenly checked the long line of spectators which had been pressing down State street,
parallel with the other body; but the rear portion,
not understanding the nature of the obstruction,
continued to press forward, and forced the front
from the sidewalk into the middle of the Street.
To the chafed and watchful military, this movement wore the aspect of an assault on the *cortege;*
instantly some Lancers, stationed near, rode their
horses furiously at the surging crowd, and hacked
with their sabres upon the defenceless heads
within their reach. Immediately after, a detachment of infantry charged upon the dense mass, at
a run, with fixed bayonets. Some were pitched
headlong down the cellar-ways, some were forced
into the passages, and up flights of stairs, and

---

[1] This remark applies not to the building, but to the spot on
which it stands. The present structure was erected in 1748.

others were overthrown upon the pavement, bruised and wounded.[1]

While this was passing, the procession moved on and reached the wharf. A breach of trust had secured to the Federal authorities the use of this wharf for their present purpose. It was the property of a company, by whom it had been committed in charge to an agent. Without their knowledge and against their wishes, he had granted to the Marshal its use on this occasion. When arraigned afterward by his employers for such betrayal of trust, he replied that he had since been rewarded by an appointment to a place in the Custom House.

At the end of the wharf lay a small steamer

[1] The assaults of the soldiers on the bystanders resulted in serious injury to several persons. One, A. L. Haskell, was attacked by Capt. Evans with a drawn sword, and cut on the back of the hand, for hissing and crying " shame." Holding up to view his bleeding hand, Mr. Haskell asked the officer his name and business. Capt. Evans gave his name, and to the inquiry touching his business, replied, " to kill just such d——d rascals as you are." A man named John Milton had his head laid open by a sabre cut, and was borne off to the hospital, where he lay for several weeks. But the most aggravated case was that of William H. Ela. While attempting to proceed quietly about his own business, he was assaulted by soldiers; beaten on the head with muskets; cut and bruised in the face; knocked down upon the pavement; and finally carried off and placed in confinement. These injuries impaired his mind to such an extent, that he was unable to go on with the business in which he was previously engaged, and which was his chief dependence for a livelihood. He afterward brought an action against Mayor Smith and others, for the assault, which became important as testing a question of law, and also as bringing to light material facts relating to the extradition of Burns.

13*

which had been chartered by the United States Government. On board this vessel Burns was conducted by the Marshal, and immediately withdrawn from the sight of the gazing thousands into the cabin below. The United States troops followed, and, after an hour's delay, the cannon was also shipped. At twenty minutes past three o'clock, the steamer left the wharf, and went down the harbor.

CHAPTER IX.

ANTHONY BURNS was born in Stafford county, Virginia. This county lies on the Potomac river, midway between the birth-place and the burial-place of Washington. Washed by one of the noblest rivers in the Union, for commercial purposes, and with an excellent soil and climate, it has not only failed to keep pace with the general prosperity of the country, but has even gone backward. In 1850, its population was nearly half a thousand less than at the close of the preceding decade; the whole number of persons, bond and free, then scattered over its surface of three hundred and thirty-five square miles, was only 8044. It has shared, perhaps, only proportionably in the decay which slavery has wrought in the whole eastern section of the Old Dominion.

The seat of justice in this little county is a village of eighty or ninety houses clustered around the Court House. At this place, twenty-three years ago, resided a slaveholder named John Suttle. He was the owner of twelve or fifteen slaves, the male portion of whom he employed in quarrying stone for the city of Washington. Among the number was

(151)

the mother of Anthony, who was employed in the family as a cook. She had been married to three husbands, by whom she had borne thirteen children, thus proving herself to be a valuable piece of property for her owner. Her last husband was a man of more than ordinary intelligence, and had been entrusted by his owner with a sort of supervision over other laborers in the quarry. It was whispered about among his fellow-bondmen that he had once been a freeman and had come from the North, but nothing was known with certainty on this point.

Anthony was this man's son and the youngest of his mother's children. Before he could remember, the death of his father, caused by inhaling the stone dust of the quarry, had occurred, and he remained as his mother's consolation. While he was yet a little child lying about the kitchen hearth, Mr. Suttle died, and his widow became the head of the family. Under her management, the estate did not prosper, and, to relieve herself from embarrassment, she sold a portion of the slaves, five of whom were the children of Burns's mother. Not long after, the family removed to Acquia, a small hamlet lying five or six miles north of Stafford Court House. This change of place did not brighten their prospects. The temper of the dame did not improve under continued adverse fortune, and in her fits of ill humor she was wont to vent her spleen upon Anthony's mother. Frequently she would threaten to sell the woman by the sale of whose children she had already been kept from bankruptcy; and at length so far carried her threat into execution as to hire her out to labor in a distant city. The mother pleaded hard for leave to take her little boy Anthony with her, but this boon was denied; the youngster might be made a source of profit at home. For two years they were not permitted to see each other. At the end of that period, Mrs. Suttle made a journey to the city to receive the wages of her slave, and on this occasion was gracious enough to take Anthony with her.

When he was about six years old, Mrs. Suttle suddenly died. The settlement of her affairs fell into the hands of her eldest son, Charles F. Suttle, who found it necessary, in order to save them from utter ruin, to mortgage the slaves and raise money for the payment of the debts. Mr. Suttle and his family held a respectable position in society, but a strict classification would not have assigned them a place among the First Families of Virginia. His business was that of a shopkeeper, to which he united that of a deputy sheriff; ultimately, he attained to the dignity of high sheriff for his county. At one time he was fortunate enough to be chosen as the representative of his district in the Virginia Assembly. To these civic distinctions were added military honors; he rose through lower grades to the post of colonel in the Virginia militia, under which designation he first became known to the great world. Of a powerful frame, well filled out, of commanding stature, and a heavy, Cass-like countenance, he was well fitted for situations which did not require intellectual so much as physical superiority.

Such was the man who now became the proprietor and master of Anthony. The boy was inured betimes to labor, but his earliest tasks were light. A wise slaveholder would as soon think of putting a six month's colt upon the race-course, as of overtaxing the tender and growing muscles of his young slaves. Anthony's juvenile contribution to his owner's annual income consisted in "nursing" his sister's baby, she being thereby left free to pursue her toil without interruption. In this capacity he accompanied her to the house of one Horton, to whom she had been hired. It was while there that he acquired the first rudiments of learning. A sister of Horton kept a school in her house hard by, and with the children attending it Anthony was frequently brought in contact. He rendered them little personal services, and in true juvenile sodality and in defiance of Virginia law, they, at his request, taught him the alphabet from a primer which one had given him.

At the age of seven, he was set to work directly to earn money for his owner, being then hired out to three maiden ladies for fifteen dollars a year. His principal duties in this new situation were to wait in the house, to run of errands, and to ride to the distant mill for a weekly supply of the indispensable corn meal. His mistresses were not unkind, and being religiously disposed, they even attempted once or twice to impart to him some knowledge of the Bible; but their efforts were too slight to produce any impression. When the year of his engagement had elapsed, he was hired to another person, living some miles distant, for twenty-five dollars a year. Another opportunity for picking up some scraps of learning was here afforded, which Anthony did not fail to improve. The wife of his new master kept a school in her house, bringing spelling-books and other educational apparatus directly before the eyes of the young slave. His thirst for knowledge was thus whetted, and by performing antics and drolleries for the amusement of the children, he induced them to teach him how to spell. What to them was an irksome task, was to him a chosen reward. In this situation he remained two years, and so well satisfied was his master with his good conduct that he made arrangements to hire him for a third year. Anthony, however, was of a different mind; he had been in some respects shabbily treated, and consequently refused to remain. In this conclusion his owner, after hearing his story, acquiesced.

He now went to live with William Brent, at Falmouth on the Rappahannock river. This man, who afterward rescued his name from obscurity by becoming a swift witness against Burns, was not at that time a person of much renown in his native region. The husband of a young lady of some fortune, he lived in her mansion, was served by her slaves, and made himself merry with eating and drinking at her expense. The chase and other

social and spendthrift pastimes constituted at that
time the business of his life. His wife was a
woman of superior endowments, and, what was
more to her credit, she treated her slaves with great
kindness. To Anthony she was especially indulgent, and he always spoke of her afterward in terms
of affection and respect. With these people he
remained two years, earning for his owner fifty
dollars each year; and so well pleased was Brent
with the bright, active young slave, that he proceeded to make a verbal agreement to hire him for
a third year. To this arrangement, however, Anthony refused his assent, agreeable as the prospect
was when measured by a slave's standard. A
more powerful motive than love of personal ease
had already begun to operate in his bosom. While
a very young boy, he had overheard the "elders"
of his people discoursing among themselves about
the good land far away to the north where no
slaves were, and where all of the negro race were
as free as their white brethren. Such conversations
had kindled a fire in his young breast that never
went out. He longed for the freedom of that far-
away land, which his untutored imagination invested with exaggerated glories. As he grew in
years, his passion for freedom also grew, and gradually, it took on the form of a definite purpose.
Then he began to cast about for the method of its
accomplishment, and his natural love of learning
received an additional stimulus from the reflection
that the more he knew of letters the better fitted

he would be to execute his cherished design. With the same end in view, he formed the resolution never to abide long with the same master, so that when he should at length flee from bondage, there might be less chance of identifying him. It was this that now led him to refuse any longer to remain with the easy and indulgent Brents.

On meeting his owner, Suttle, near the close of the year, the latter greeted him with compliments.

" Well, 'Tony, Mr. Brent speaks very well of you. He likes you so well that he has hired you for another year."

" But, Mas'r Charles, I have n't hired *him*," said Anthony, with the confident tone of a slave conscious of standing well with his master.

" What 's the matter ? Has n't he treated you well ? "

" Yes, mas'r, but — " Some reason, though of course not the real one, was assigned.

" Well, it can't be helped now, for I 've agreed to let you stop with Mr. Brent; and besides, he pays more for you than he did last year."

" Jes' you say, mas'r. The *woods* is big enough to hold me."

The *argumentum a sylva* is a prevailing one with the slaveholder. Col. Suttle yielded, and the bargain was broken up. He knew that it was better for his own interest to humor his slave in the choice of his field of labor, than to run the risk of trouble and loss by thwarting his inclinations. Long and sore experience has taught the enlightened slave-

14

holders of the south, that one willing slave is worth half-a-dozen refractory ones. Having defeated his owner's arrangement, Anthony was now ordered to present himself on the "hiring-ground" and find a new master.

The impoverished condition of Virginia has engendered a peculiar custom, not found, — certainly not to the same extent, — in the less exhausted states of the south. Many slaveholders, having upon their hands more slaves than employment for them, make a practice of hiring them out to other persons needing their services. For this purpose, they are often sent long distances from their owner's estate, and members of the same family are scattered wide asunder. The contracts are made for only a single year. The time for hiring is during the Christmas holidays. Some convenient point is selected — at the Court House or some large village — where the owners and their slaves assemble to arrange the matter. This is called the hiring-ground, and, as it remains the same from year to year, it becomes familiarly known to the slaves in the region round about. An owner living ten, twenty, or even thirty miles distant, has, it may be, come to the conclusion to hire out a number of his slaves. He summons the whole body before him, designates several by name, and orders them to meet him on the hiring-ground at a specified hour of perhaps the next day. He then directs them to procure passes at the office and dismisses them. They are now left to find their way to the hiring-ground on foot, whatever the distance; and it is at their peril if they fail to appear at the appointed time. While there, — sometimes for several days, — they are left to shift for themselves. The owner provides them with neither food nor shelter at night; a small piece of silver, bestowed upon each, is the extent of the means which he places at their disposal. If they are not fortunate enough to find shelter in the cabin of some friendly slave in the neighborhood, they build a fire in the street or in the field, and, gathering around, pass the night in the open air.

During the season of negotiation, the hiring-ground exhibits a busy spectacle. Hundreds are present, all intent upon one common business. The slave plays an important part in the transaction. He must be as active as his owner in finding some one to hire him. He is expected to praise himself without stint, and to give assurance to all inquirers that he is able to perform any sort of labor. Often it happens that a person comes in search of a slave qualified for some particular service, perchance that of coachman. His eye lights upon one looking more than usually trim, and he accosts him:

"Whose boy are you?"

The slave informs him.

"What can you do?"

The slave enumerates several kinds of employment with which he may have been familiar.

" Can you drive a coach and take the management and care of horses?"

The slave is, it may be, totally ignorant of such business; but, if he fears his owner's displeasure, he will promptly answer that he can. If he fears God (as some do) and speaks the truth, he knows well that stripes are likely to be his reward. Sometimes the owner stands by and answers for him, — falsely, it may be. When a bargain is made, the parties retire to execute it in writing. Besides the sum of money agreed upon, the contract usually stipulates that the person hiring shall provide the slave with a hat or cap, a pair of shoes, and two suits of clothes during the year. Of all these stipulations the slave is always well informed. When the transaction is completed, he is turned over to his new master, who orders him to appear at his house on a specified day. He may be indulged with a day or two more on the hiring-ground, but from thence, without returning home, he goes directly to his new field of service.

Most of the slaves belonging to Col. Suttle were subjected to this system of hiring, and thus it happened that Anthony, from his earliest years, was never much under his owner's eye. After the conversation relating to service with Brent, he repaired to the hiring-ground and soon fell in with a person named Foote, who was attracted by his appearance. The attraction was not mutual, and Anthony did not manifest much alacrity in satisfying Foote's inquiries. Col. Suttle stood by; and when

Foote asked Anthony what he could do, replied for him with some sternness:

" He can do *anything*."

It happened that Foote was in search of a boy to tend a steam engine in his saw-mill, and to this new and strange business the young and inexperienced slave felt a natural aversion. But his owner was not disposed to humor him a second time, and a bargain was concluded by which seventy-five dollars were to be paid for his services. Foote dwelt in the edge of Culpepper, bordering on Stafford county, and thither Anthony now went. He was at this time twelve or thirteen years of age.

The new home did not prove to be very agreeable. Foote and his wife were Yankees, and they presented no exception to the classification which assigns to apostates from northern principles of freedom a place among the severest taskmasters of the south. Young slaves scarcely three feet high were beaten by the mistress without mercy. Strapped upon a plank with their faces downward, they were belabored with an instrument of torture peculiar to slave-land, consisting of a strip of board perforated with holes and roughened with tar and sand. The air, drawn through the holes as the board smote upon the skin, would raise blisters, while the sand increased the smart without deeply cutting up the flesh and thereby diminishing the market value of the slave. Besides cruelties of this sort, the most niggardly fare was doled out, and occasionally, in a fit of gloomy merriment,

14*

Anthony would hold up to the sun his thin shaving of meat to show what a transparent humbug it was. His lot, however, was not one of unmixed evil, for, through the friendly teaching of a young daughter of his employer, he was enabled to make some further progress in his cherished pursuit of knowledge.

When he had been two or three months in the service of Foote, an accident of a serious nature befell him. He was busy about the discharge of his duties in the mill, when Foote, without giving him warning, set the machinery in motion, and Anthony's hand was caught by a wheel and shockingly mangled.[1] This accident laid him aside from work for two months. He returned to Falmouth, where Col. Suttle then had a sheriff's office, and in this was provided with a lodging until he was able to resume his toil. On meeting his owner, he pointed to his broken hand, and significantly remarked, " That's ' *anything.*' " Col. Suttle did not relish this taunting allusion to his former recommendation of Burns on the hiring-ground.

During this period of suffering and exemption from labor, occurred the crisis in Anthony's religious history. He had been the subject of strong religious impressions from early childhood. His mother, who was a devout woman, had tried to

---

[1] The scar, or rather protruding broken bone, which disfigured his hand after the wound had healed, was commonly, but of course erroneously supposed, during his examination, to have resulted from abusive treatment by his master.

tell him something about God. He had been excited by the fervors of the camp-meeting. About the same time, the doctrines of Millerism had penetrated the little obscure Virginia county, and filled all hearts with alarm. It became the universal topic; white and black shared alike in the excitement. The barriers of class and caste were, for the time, thrown down, and never before had there been such unreserved communication between master and slave. To this was added a real cause of alarm; the scarlet fever swept over the district, leaving fearful ravages in its path. The young mind of Anthony shared in the general excitement produced by these unwonted causes, and he earnestly set about a preparation for the future life. He would retire into the recesses of the forest to pray, but there no light shone in upon him. Extravagant hopes and terrors alternately possessed him. At one time he looked momently to see Jesus appear in bodily shape before him; at another, believing that he actually saw the Fiend in the form of a serpent, he would spring from the ground, and with frantic outcries rush from the forest. Gradually, his extreme religious excitement subsided, but he never lost the sense of spiritual need. In this condition he remained until the accident occurred which has been already recorded.

Impelled by bodily anguish, and fearing that his injury might terminate fatally, he applied himself with renewed earnestness to the Friend of the afflicted. All at once a thought flashed through his mind: — "Here have I been praying to Jesus, whom I have never served, and have never thought of praying to the Devil, whom I have always served." This was a new revelation. He saw it was unreasonable to expect help from a Being whose service he had not entered. He saw that repentance and reformation of life were the first steps for him to take. Thus put upon the right path by the Infinite Spirit working with his spirit, he soon found the help and peace that he sought.

After a suitable lapse of time, he applied to Col. Suttle, according to custom, for leave to be baptized; no slave being suffered to comply with that command of the Saviour or admitted to the church without a written permission from his owner. To Anthony's request, Col. Suttle, irritated by the prospect of loss from the maimed hand, returned a rough refusal, and even added words to wound the spirit of the young convert. If he joined the church, Suttle said, he would soon be drinking or following the women, like others. Anthony turned away with a heavy heart, but still with a silent resolve to pray that God would yet incline his owner to grant his request. The prayer was answered. Returning some time after from Foote's, where he had again resumed his labor in the mill, he unexpectedly met his owner in a carriage, on his way to the Springs. The latter kindly saluted him, and now of his own accord gave the requisite permission for baptism. Emboldened by such rare favor, Anthony petitioned for money to buy clothes in which to appear with decency on the occasion of taking his baptismal vows, and received two dollars, —sixteen-fold more than Col. Suttle ever gave him at any one time, before or after.

At the proper time he was baptized and received into the Baptist church at Falmouth. The church consisted of white freemen and black slaves. All assembled within the same walls for worship on the Sabbath, but a partition of boards separated the bond from the free. When the Holy Supper was administered, the cup was first carefully served to all of the privileged class, and afterward to their sable brethren. Those distinctions were not maintained in anticipation of heaven, but in deference to the prejudices of Virginia society. In the social religious meetings there was a somewhat nearer approach to the New Testament model, and the prayers and exhortations of the slaves were graciously suffered to intermingle with those proceeding from the master's lips.

Among the Christian slaves at the south there is a class of persons that bear the character of quasi-pastors or preachers. Without being formally set apart to the sacred office by any rite of ordination, they yet receive a sort of recognition from the church with which they may happen to be connected. Piety, a gift at exhortation, and a desire for the work of a preacher, are the requisite qualifications. All these were found in Anthony when, at the end of two years from the period of his baptism, he applied to his brethren for their recognition

of him as a preacher. A day was appointed when
he should exhibit his gifts to the assembled members of the church. Sitting around with ears more
than usually critical, yet not without sympathy,
they listened while Anthony addressed to them an
exhortation from the desk. His effort proved satisfactory, and, at the close, pastor and brethren,
taking him by the hand, bade him God speed.
Thenceforth he exercised his new office as he had
opportunity. Gathering a little congregation of
slaves, sometimes in the kitchen of a friendly
white person, sometimes in the rude cabin of a
slave, he would lead them in their devotions and
speak to them of the Gospel. These meetings,
however, as well as all other assemblies consisting
exclusively of slaves, were violations of Virginia
law. Every such assembly, unless sanctioned by the
presence of a white, was exposed to rude interruption, and the slaves that might be caught, to severe
punishment. The patrols and guards that nightly
walked their rounds were constantly on the watch
to detect these secret meetings, and, in spite of all
caution, they would occasionally succeed. Perhaps
while the assembly were in the act of prayer, the
door would be suddenly burst open by a throng of
profane officials, each with cord in hand, bent on
securing as many victims as possible. When
such surprisals occurred, the first movement would
be to extinguish the lights; then, through door,
window, and even chimney, the affrighted wor-
shippers hurried their escape. Those who were

unlucky enough to be caught, were taken to the cage,[1] and the next day rewarded with nine-and-thirty lashes at the whipping post for having peacefully, but unlawfully, assembled to worship God. Anthony was not without experience of this sort, though he was always so fortunate as to escape from the clutches of the officers.

In his new capacity, it sometimes fell to his lot to perform the marriage rite for slaves, or what among them was called such; and sometimes to conduct the burial service for the dead. If a slave died during the week, no funeral was allowed to interrupt the daily toil of the plantation. The body, encased perchance in an orange-box, was deposited in the ground without ceremony or delay, and a few shovelfulls of earth were thrown in, while the bereaved kindred went about their toil as usual. But on the following Sabbath, the whole body of the slaves, attended by the master or the overseer, assembled to "sod the grave." With prayers, exhortations, and much singing of hymns, in the sad, wild negro airs, this final ceremony was completed.

In death as in life, the social distinctions of slavery are carefully maintained. Laid to rest in a "potter's field," the dead bodies of the slaves never mingle their dust with that of the sovereign race. No monument, inscribed with the name of the deceased, ever marks the spot where he lies, as

[1] A place provided everywhere in towns at the South, for the temporary confinement of delinquent slaves.

no legal sanction was ever given to his name while he lived. A rough stone, gathered from the way-side, or a branch of cedar, soon to die, is his only monument. So perish, an undistinguishable throng, the enslaved race of the South. For two centuries the long and ever swelling procession has been moving on in its weary path to the grave, but no name of them all survive, save where, here and there, one has escaped out of the American Egypt, or, Spartacus-like, has risen to take bloody vengeance on his oppressors. A race of many millions has mingled in the very thick of American civilization reaching even into the nineteenth century, and yet their place in human history is a blank.

When Anthony had ended his year of service with Foote, he found a new master in Falmouth. This man, not having employment enough for him, re-let him at the end of six months to a wholesale merchant. The latter proved to be a harsh master, and Anthony refused to remain beyond the expiration of his time, much to the merchant's disappointment. With the new year, he entered the service of a tavern-keeper in Fredericksburg. The annual income which his owner derived from his services had now risen to one hundred dollars, notwithstanding the drawback caused by his lame hand. At the end of the year, true to his secret purpose of frequently changing his place, he sought and obtained a new situation in the establishment of an apothecary in Fredericksburg. While there, an incident occurred that made all his hopes of freedom to bud and blossom afresh. Going into the kitchen of his employer one day, he found there a fortune-teller who at once beset him to cross her palm with his shilling. With some reluctance Anthony consented, and the woman proceeded to flatter him with the usual nonsense about love. But Anthony waited with secret anxiety to hear if she would prophesy to him of freedom; and when at length she *did* promise him that long dreamed of bliss, he almost fainted with the rush of emotion. Not content with uttering an indefinite prediction, she even fixed the period when he should become a freeman, and fixed it only a few months forward. Was it strange that a slave, panting to breathe the air of liberty, should catch at such a straw? With increasing restlessness he looked forward to the predicted time. When it had passed and he still remained in slavery as before, his faith in fortune-telling was naturally staggered. But a change in his circumstances occurred about this time that contributed to keep alive, and even to strengthen, his hopes.

Col. Suttle had hitherto managed the hiring of his own slaves; he now appointed William Brent his agent for that purpose. The latter having at length discovered that work and not sport is the law of life, had removed from Falmouth to Richmond and entered the service of his brother-in-law as a clerk. He now sent for Anthony for the purpose of hiring him out in the latter city. This was welcome intelligence, for, besides placing him in a community where he was unknown, the change would bring him to the very side of the ships that might help him wing his way to the North. Accordingly, at the close of the year, he set out for the metropolis of Virginia, having under his charge four other slaves belonging to Col. Suttle, also bound for the hiring-ground.

The trust committed to him on this occasion was but one proof of the high place which Anthony held in his owner's esteem. As he had grown up, his superiority, natural and acquired, to the other slaves of Col. Suttle, had become more and more manifest, and in the end he was made a supervisor over the whole. He found them new masters at the end of the year; if anything went amiss with them, it was to him that the owner or his agent looked for an account. Once a year, there was a re-union of Col. Suttle and all his slaves. The scene was a little cabin in Stafford where Anthony's mother, now verging upon fourscore, and his sister, a breeding-woman, had their quarters. To this centre, the hired slaves, under the superintendence of Anthony, were required to repair at the close of the year, however distant they might be. The owner met them, saw for himself their personal condition, and received reports of what had transpired in respect to themselves. If any had been sick, or had fallen into difficulties with their employers, or had been punished by the authorities, this was the time for explanation. The interview ended with a dotation from Col. Suttle of a dime, or some other small coin, to each. Usually, this was the only time in the year when he and his slaves met each other face to face.

On arriving in Richmond, Anthony found that a master had already been provided for himself in the person of Brent's brother-in-law. A day's acquaintance satisfied him that they would never get on harmoniously together, and he refused his assent to the arrangement. In the mean time, he busied himself with providing situations for the slaves that had been placed in his charge. Having accomplished this, he then found a place for himself with the proprietor of a large flouring establishment where an elder brother was already employed. All being thus happily provided for by the enterprise and address of Anthony, nothing remained for the agent Brent but to execute the contracts in writing.

Meanwhile he had continued to make progress in his education. At Acquia, in Culpepper, in Falmouth, and in Fredericksburg, he had found one and another to assist him in the struggle. The spelling-book had been mastered, and the New Testament had begun to yield up its meaning to his patient application. At length he essayed a bolder flight. A part of his business had usually been to fetch his master's letters from the post-office. One day the thought struck him that if he were able to write, he too might send letters to his friends, and no one be the wiser. He resolved, if it were possible, to learn the precious art. He gathered from the street some torn scraps of paper with writing upon them, and carefully imitated the characters. These rude copies he ventured to show to a young lady whom he had known as a child at Miss Horton's school. His confidence was not misplaced; although contrary to Virginia law, she kindly explained their meaning and lent him further aid. Thus, by the time he arrived in Richmond, he was already able to read and to write with a considerable degree of correctness. Such unusual attainments gave him a position in that city which he did not fail to improve to his own advantage, as well as that of others. He set up a school for the instruction of slaves — old as well as young — in reading. When the labors of the day were over, he was wont to meet twelve or fifteen in the house of a free negro woman for that purpose. This practice he continued for several months, and while it directly promoted his mental improvement, it was also a source of pecuniary profit.

At the end of his first year in Richmond, he changed his masters for the last time. His new employer was a druggist named Millspaugh. In about a week after Anthony had entered upon his new engagement, Millspaugh took him aside, and proposed a different arrangement. He had expected, he said, to have had employment enough to keep Anthony constantly busy, but found that such was not the case, and that he was likely to lose money by retaining him. He proposed, therefore, that Anthony should take the matter into his

own hands on these conditions: That he should
pay to Millspaugh the sum ($125), which Col.
Suttle was to receive, that he should clothe himself, and, finally, that he should pay Millspaugh a
bonus, the amount of which was left to Anthony's
generosity.   He was to seek jobs here and there in
the city, and every evening pay to his master a
certain sum from his earnings.   This arrangement,
Millspaugh informed him, was in violation of law,
and must of course be kept secret; nor, as Anthony understood, was it ever made known to
Suttle or to Brent.   He joyfully accepted the
proposal, and with new springs of life went forth
to seek work, which had thus suddenly become his
best friend.   It soon appeared, however, that the
arrangement to pay Millspaugh every night would
be inconvenient, and even impossible, since his
daily earnings were variable, and on some days he
had failed of a job altogether.   It was therefore
arranged that he should make a payment to his
master at the end of every fortnight.

All this while, the great purpose of his life had
had been fast ripening for action.   He had now
dwelt a year in the midst of circumstances that
strongly fostered its developement.   He was in
daily sight of those northern keels that seemed
to him a part of the very soil of freedom.   He was
in daily converse with men whose birthright was
in a free land, and whose language to the slave
had no smack of the whip.   Kindhearted sailors,
having no vessels to forfeit, and no trade to com-

promise, did not hesitate to urge him on to flight. Plainly, the time was at hand, when, if ever, he was to achieve his freedom.

One very serious obstacle lay in his path, and must be overcome. As already narrated, he had become a member of the church, and more than that, a preacher of the gospel. Was it right for him to run away from his owner? The question troubled him. He could not bring reproach upon the sacred cause he had espoused; if he fled from slavery, it must be with a clear conscience. To resolve his doubts, he searched the Scriptures. He fell upon the Epistle to Philemon, which has furnished so much comfort to pious slaveholders, and, strangely enough, it relieved and comforted Anthony also. For he read that though Paul had sent back a runaway slave, it was that he should be no longer a slave, but a brother beloved unto his former master. Still pursuing his investigations, he met with the case of the bond-woman Hagar, whom, when she had fled from hard usage, the angel of the Lord had commanded to return and become submissive to her mistress. This seemed to contradict the principle inculcated by Paul, and in his perplexity Anthony applied to others for light. They summarily expounded the passage as a divine sanction to the slave code of the Old Dominion. Not satisfied — as how could he be with what would wither his now brightly blooming hopes — Anthony searched further, and reflected with deeper earnestness. As the result of his inquiries, he found that the Bible set forth only one God for the black and the white races, that He had made of one blood all the nations of the earth, that there was no divine ordinance requiring one part of the human family to be in bondage to another, and that there was no passage of Holy Writ by virtue of which Col. Suttle could claim a right of property in him, any more than he could in Col. Suttle. These considerations ended his doubts. Paul was on his side, the whole spirit of the Gospel sanctioned his desires, and he deliberately dismissed Hagar from his thoughts. From that moment, with a clear conscience and full integrity of Christian character, he applied himself to the recovery of his inalienable right to liberty and the pursuit of happiness.

The new arrangement for paying Millspaugh was highly favorable to the success of his plans. So long as he was required to reckon every night, there was little chance of making good his escape. His failure to appear would have been remarked by his expectant master, and continued absence would have been followed by speedy search. But now, he was not expected until the end of a fortnight; nor would suspicion be excited if he were not seen during that interval. A fortnight's start in the race for freedom was, under ordinary circumstances, more than enough to place him upon the soil of New England, and it was his. This fair prospect was suddenly obscured. At the end of the first month, Anthony paid to his master twenty-five dollars, showing that he was earning at the rate of three hundred dollars a year. This fact seemed to put a new thought into Millspaugh's head. He revoked his permission for settlements once a fortnight, and not only required them to be made daily, as at first, but also required that the whole sum of one hundred and twenty-five dollars should be paid as fast as possible. Did he design, when that was paid, to ignore the unlawful bargain with his slave, and appropriate his earnings for the remainder of the year? Whatever his secret purpose, it was effectually baulked. Anthony strenuously objected to the arrangement, and finally left Millspaugh's presence without giving his consent. But he saw that the crisis had come, and he proceeded to act accordingly.

On becoming master of his own time, according to the arrangement with Millspaugh, he had sought and obtained employment on the vessels lying at the wharves. Much of the time, he was on board assisting to discharge cargoes of coals, guano, and other lading. He was thus brought into familiar intercourse with the sailors, and with one in particular he was soon on the most confidential terms. The subject of his bondage was broached, and his aspirations for freedom were disclosed. The sympathetic sailor entered heartily into his views, and a plan for his escape had already been concerted, when Millspaugh's change of purpose suddenly precipitated its execution. Although Anthony had refused his assent to the new arrangement, yet he had every reason to fear that it would be enforced notwithstanding his remonstrances. He would thus be required to appear daily in his master's presence. But he imagined that for the first few days his failure to do so would naturally be attributed to his reluctance on this point, and so suspicion would be disarmed. This precious interval he now resolved should witness his departure from slave-land.

At the very last, a sharp struggle awaited him. Love, which does not discriminate between black and white, bond and free, had made a conquest of Anthony. He had formed an attachment to a bond-woman of his own race, and there was before him a bright prospect of soon enjoying the highest solace which slave life affords. To sunder this tender tie was hard, but to forego the prospect of liberty was harder still. Besides, his desire for freedom had by this time assumed a high moral character; as a Christian man, his soul was fettered; as one seeking to benefit his fellow-men, he found himself under restraints too great to be borne. The higher motive triumphed, love was sacrificed on the altar of liberty.

The third night after his last interview with Millspaugh was fixed upon for putting his purpose into execution; it was one of the early days in February, 1854. His lodging-place was in Millspaugh's house, directly over that person's chamber. Gathering some few effects into a small bundle, he encased himself in four suits of clothes — the

outer suit being the coarse garb in which he performed his daily toil — and lay down to pass a
sleepless night.   In the same room, a roguish young
negro boy was accustomed to sleep, by whom
there was danger that his strange plight would be
discovered.   Fortunately, no detection took place.
An hour before daylight, he rose and took his way
about a mile to the wharves.   Had he found any
persons around, it was his purpose to have gone
to work as usual.   Finding the coast clear, he
rapidly passed on board the vessel to which his
sailor-friend belonged, and was quickly stowed
away in a place of concealment previously prepared by the latter.

The vessel did not sail that day, as had been
expected, and, while she still lay at the wharf, sleep
fell upon Anthony, already exhausted by watching.
When he again awoke, she was ten or fifteen miles
down the river, under full sail.   Contrary winds
retarded the voyage, and the roughened waters
caused the vessel to pitch and toss at an unusual
rate.   The effect produced upon Anthony's physical system was too much for his endurance.   Shut
up in a dark hole, where he was compelled to lie
constantly in one position, and left for several days
without a morsel of food, he had to undergo, in
addition, the pangs of sea-sickness, redoubled by
the other miseries of his situation, and by their
very strangeness.   In his extreme misery, he entreated his friend to put him on shore and leave
him to his fate; but this was impossible.   At the

end of two days the vessel reached Norfolk, where she lay to for a short time, and then resumed her voyage for Boston. The ordinary time for the passage was from ten to fourteen days, but for three weeks Anthony was tossed upon the ocean before he again set foot on land. During all that time he never once left his narrow hiding-place, nor was he able to change his position in the least degree. Lying constantly on one side, he for a time entirely lost the use of his right arm. Bread and water were his only nourishment, and these he received only at intervals of three or four days, as his friend found opportunity to convey them to him by stealth. For, from first to last, neither the captain nor any officer was aware of his being on board. As the vessel passed into the more northern latitudes, he was assailed by a degree of cold such as his southern life had ill fitted him to endure, and, before the voyage was ended, his feet were frozen stiff in his boots.

At length, somewhere in the last days of February or first of March, the vessel touched her wharf at Boston. Seizing a favorable opportunity, Anthony succeeded in getting on shore unobserved. It was in the gray of the morning, and few people were moving. Assuming the air of a seaman, he inquired his way to a boarding-house, and was soon provided for. A week elapsed before he was sufficiently recovered of his bruises to move about with any comfort. He then sought for employment, and at length secured the situation of a cook on board a mud-scow. In the discharge of his new duties everything succeeded satisfactorily but one — he was unable to make his bread rise. This was a fatal defect, and at the end of a week he was discharged. His next permanent employment was that in which he was found by the slave-hunter.[1] I now resume the narrative of his extradition.

[1] The discovery of his place of refuge was made by means of a letter which he wrote to his brother in Richmond, and which he had incautiously dated at Boston, while taking care to have it postmarked in Canada. It of course first fell into the hands of his brother's master, who communicated the contents to Brent or Suttle.

CHAPTER X.

THE TRADER'S JAIL.

A SHORT distance down the harbor, the United States revenue cutter was lying to, in readiness to receive its prey. Col. Suttle and his witness Brent were already on board. Their absence from the court-room, at the rendering of the decision, had been remarked; the more, as it was in striking contrast with their sedulous attendance on all the previous days of the trial. It was afterward ascertained that they had quietly left their hotel at early dawn on the same morning, passed over to the Navy Yard at Charlestown, and from thence had been transported with their baggage to the revenue cutter. That the claimant of Burns should thus calmly turn his back upon the court in the very crisis of his cause, that the commander of a national vessel should thus place it at the service of a private citizen without any ostensible warrant, were significant facts. The public placed but one construction upon the proceeding; they saw in it conclusive proof that the Commissioner had privately made known his decision to one of the interested parties before he declared it in open court.

The steamer was soon placed alongside the cut-

16 (181)

ter, to which Burns was immediately transferred, together with Deputy Marshal Riley, Butman, and four others, who had been detailed to escort the slave back to Virginia. The cutter was then taken in tow by the steamer, and together they passed down the harbor. At the end of a few miles, the two vessels cast loose from each other, a parting salute was fired, and the steamer returned to disembark the soldiers and cannon, while the cutter pursued its solitary course for Virginia.

On entering the cabin of the cutter, Anthony found himself once more face to face with Col. Suttle. " How do you do, 'Tony? " was the latter's salutation. A private conference between Col. Suttle and the Marshal ensued, during which Butman and others were banished from the cabin. After the departure of the Marshal, Col. Suttle proceeded to interrogate Burns respecting his escape. He offered to give him his freedom, if he would divulge the name of the captain who brought him off from Virginia. To disarm and conciliate Burns, he prefaced his question with a testimony to the truthfulness of the latter.

" This boy," said he to the bystanders, " has always been an honest, upright servant, and I have never known him to tell a lie."

To the demand for the captain's name, Burns replied, simply and truthfully, " I do not know it."

Thereupon Col. Suttle, in the face of his previous testimony, expressed a doubt of his truthfulness. But Burns persisted then, and ever after-

ward, in asserting his ignorance of the captain's
name. It had never been a matter of curiosity
with him; he had never seen the captain while on
board his ship, and probably not at any other time.
Failing to obtain any light from Anthony, Col.
Suttle gave vent to his vindictive feelings toward
the unknown and really innocent captain.

" If I knew the scoundrel," said he, " he would n't
want to bring off another negro. I would put him
in the Penitentiary for life."

" He ought to be," responded the zealous Butman; and he added that on arriving at Richmond
he thought he should be able to find him out.

A slight incident showed that those by whom
Burns was surrounded regarded him with no
friendly spirit. On taking up his hat, which he
had laid aside, he found in it a letter. He forthwith took it to Col. Suttle, explaining to him the
circumstances under which it had been found. It
proved to contain a written speech purporting to
have been delivered by Burns against Col. Suttle
and the laws of the land. The author was never
discovered; his object plainly was to prejudice
Col. Suttle against the friendless fugitive.

During the voyage, Anthony had abundant leis-
ure for reflection. Uncertainty respecting the fate
that awaited him weighed down his spirits and
filled him with fears. Would he be whipped?
Would he be imprisoned? Would he be sold and
sent to the far South? Would his life be sacri-

ficed? Once, when Col. Suttle was sitting upon deck, he approached and said:

" Master Charles, what are you going to do with me?"

" What do you think I *ought* to do, 'Tony?"

" I expect you will sell me."

Col. Suttle replied that Anthony had caused him great expense, that his lawyers' fees alone had been four hundred dollars; but he left unanswered the slave's anxious inquiry.

On arriving at a point off New York Bay, the cutter fell in with a steamer bound for that city. By this time, Suttle and Brent had become thoroughly seasick, and they improved the opportunity to leave the cutter, intending to make the remainder of their journey overland. After their departure, the situation of Anthony became less agreeable. He had hitherto enjoyed the freedom of the vessel; now he was restricted to a certain part of it. He was required to take his meals by himself. No one looked kindly upon him but the sailors that manned the vessel. The departure of Col. Suttle was also the signal for Butman and his coadjutors to beset Anthony afresh. They importuned him to tell them the whole matter, now that it was ended; and they were especially curious to ascertain if the witnesses in behalf of Burns had told the truth. Again they renewed their protestations of friendship; in proof of it, they reminded Anthony that it was they who had procured for him new clothes and supplied him with money. They at length proceeded to tempt him with a proposition in full keeping with the infamy of their own course. They assured him that they would procure his immediate freedom, provided he would return and assist them in catching fugitive slaves. To strengthen the lure, they informed him that one negro in Boston had engaged in the business, and grown rich by so doing. But Burns understood his men, and was fully proof against their machinations.

" You wish," said he, " to get out of me all that you can, for the purpose of injuring my friends in Massachusetts, and then you will leave me to die in Virginia. I know I am green; but, mark me, I am ripe enough for you in this matter."

On Saturday, after a voyage of eight days, the vessel arrived at Norfolk. Informed by telegraph of Burns's departure from Boston, the Virginia city was already awaiting his appearance. Although Richmond was the destination of the fugitive, yet Norfolk was determined to share in the triumph of her sister city. On two former occasions she had been baulked in her attempts to recover fugitives from Massachusetts on her own account, and the failure had only increased her eagerness.[1] Accordingly, as the vessel drew to land, the officers of the city went on board and taking possession of Anthony, carried

[1] Latimer, whom Gov. Davis declined to surrender to the Governor of Virginia in 1843, when requisition was made on the false pretence that he was a fugitive from *justice*, and Shadrach, who was the first fugitive slave arrested in Massachusetts after the passage of the Act of 1850, and who made good his escape from the officer, — were both Norfolk slaves.

16*

him off to the jail.   A crowd followed them
through the streets, anxious to catch a glimpse of
the " Boston Lion," as their excited imaginations
led them to style him.   He was thrown into the
common jail, where he was kept in solitude for
two days, without bed or seat, and with only a
single meal during the whole period.   It was the
first greeting which slave-land gave to its recovered
slave — starvation in prison.   On Monday, the
voyage was resumed, and the same day Burns was
landed on the wharf at the capital of Virginia.

It was expected that Brent would meet the party
on their arrival in Richmond, but he failed to make
his appearance.   They therefore took a carriage
and were driven immediately to the principal hotel
of the city.   There the deputy marshal and his
aids took lodgings, but Burns was delivered into
the custody of an officer, by whom he was forthwith
lodged in the common jail for safe keeping.

The Federal Government had at length performed the task which it had undertaken.   A vast
amount of money had been expended; time, human
life, the national reputation, and the law of nature
had been sacrificed in order to restore a single slave
to his master: but it was thought that the political
well-being of the nation required it all.   The result
demonstrated that the fugitive slave act was the
most costly, as it was the most infamous, upon the
statute-book; and it produced the certain conviction that the next attempt to execute it in the

Commonwealth of Massachusetts would prove more costly still.

In the jail, Anthony remained uncared for during ten days. He was indulged with the freedom of the jail-yard and no task was assigned him. A moderate allowance of coarse food, twice a day, was all that he had to satisfy his hunger. On being incarcerated, his person was searched and his knife and some money were taken from him. These were never restored, southern jailers not disdaining to rob even slaves of their small possessions. At the end of ten days, Brent presented himself at the jail. He was in no gracious mood. Incidentally, he had been informed that Anthony had denied to some persons having any acquaintance with him. To be ignored by a slave under his own charge was too much for the equanimity of Mr. Brent, and, on first meeting Anthony, he compromised his dignity by betraying the cause of his spleen. The ruffled feathers were smoothed by a quiet denial of the absurd accusation on the part of Burns.

Brent was accompanied to the jail by one Robert Lumpkin, a noted trader in slaves. This man belonged to a class of persons by whose society the slaveholders of the South profess to feel disgraced, but with whose services, nevertheless, they cannot dispense. He had formerly been engaged exclusively in the traffic in slaves. Roaming over the country, and picking up a husband here, a wife there, a mother in one place, and an alluring maiden in another, he banded them with iron links into a coffle and sent them to the far southern market. By his ability and success in this remorseless business, he had greatly distinguished himself, and had come to be known as a " bully trader." At this time, however, he had abandoned the business of an itinerant trader, and was established in Richmond as the proprietor of a Trader's Jail. In this he kept and furnished with board such slaves as were brought into the city for sale, and, generally, all such as their owners wished to punish or to provide with temporary safe keeping. He also kept a boarding-house for the owners themselves. Lumpkin's Jail was one of the prominent and characteristic features of the capital of Virginia. It was a large brick structure, three stories in height, situated in the outskirts of Richmond, and surrounded by an acre of ground. The whole was enclosed by a high, close fence, the top of which was thickly set with iron spikes.

To the proprietor of this prison, Burns was now delivered up by Brent. He was ordered by Lumpkin to put his hands behind him; this done, the jail-keeper proceeded to fasten them together in that position with a pair of iron handcuffs. Then, directing Anthony to move on before, he followed him closely behind until they arrived at his jail.

Here he was destined to suffer, for four months, such revolting treatment as the vilest felons never undergo, and such as only revengeful slaveholders can inflict. The place of his confinement was a

room only six or eight feet square, in the upper
story of the jail, which was accessible only through
a trap-door. He was allowed neither bed nor
chair; a rude bench fastened against the wall and
a single coarse blanket were the only means of re-
pose. After entering his cell, the handcuffs were
not removed, but, in addition, fetters were placed
upon his feet. In this manacled condition he was
kept during the greater part of his confinement.
The torture which he suffered, in consequence, was
excruciating. The gripe of the irons impeded the
circulation of his blood, made hot and rapid by
the stifling atmosphere, and caused his feet to swell
enormously. The flesh was worn from his wrists,
and when the wounds had healed, there remained
broad scars as perpetual witnesses against his owner.
The fetters also prevented him from removing his
clothing by day or night, and no one came to help
him; the indecency resulting from such a condition
is too revolting for description, or even thought.
His room became more foul and noisome than the
hovel of a brute; loathsome creeping things multiplied and rioted in the filth. His food consisted
of a piece of coarse corn-bread and the parings of
bacon or putrid meat. This fare, supplied to him
once a day, he was compelled to devour without
plate, knife, or fork. Immured, as he was, in a
narrow, unventilated room, beneath the heated roof
of the jail, a constant supply of fresh water would
have been a heavenly boon; but the only means
of quenching his thirst was the nauseating contents

of a pail that was replenished only once or twice
a week. Living under such an accumulation of
atrocities, he at length fell seriously ill. This
brought about some mitigation of his treatment;
his fetters were removed for a time, and he was
supplied with broth, which, compared with his previous food, was luxury itself.

When first confined in the jail, he became an
object of curiosity to all who had heard of his case,
and twenty or thirty persons in a day would call to
gaze upon him. On these occasions, his fetters
were taken off and he was conducted down to the
piazza in front of the jail. His visitors improved
the opportunity to express their opinion of his
deserts; having no pecuniary interest in his life,
they were anxious that it should be sacrificed for
the general good of slaveholders. When curiosity
was satisfied, he would be led back to his cell, and
again placed in irons. These exhibitions occurred
ordinarily once a day during the first two or three
weeks, and, though humiliating, furnished a relief
to the solitude of his confinement. There were
other slaves in the jail, who were allowed more or
less intercourse with each other; but between them
and Burns all communication was strictly prohibited. The taint of freedom was upon him, and
infection was dreaded.

His residence in the jail gave him an opportunity of gaining new views of the system of slavery.
One day his attention was attracted by a noise in
the room beneath him. There was a sound as of

a woman entreating and sobbing, and of a man
addressing to her commands mingled with oaths.
Looking down through a crevice in the floor,
Burns beheld a slave woman stark naked in the
presence of two men. One of them was an overseer, and the other a person who had come to purchase a slave. The overseer had compelled the
woman to disrobe in order that the purchaser might
see for himself whether she was well formed and
sound in body. Burns was horror-stricken; all
his previous experience had not made him aware
of such an outrage. This, however, was not an
exceptional case; he found it was the ordinary
custom in Lumpkin's jail thus to expose the naked
person of the slave, both male and female, to the
inspection of the purchaser. A wider range of
observation would have enabled him to see that it
was the universal custom in the slave states.

In spite of the interdict under which he was laid,
Burns found a method of communicating with
other slaves in the jail. It has been stated that
during his illness he was released from his fetters
and supplied with broth. The spoon given him to
eat with, on that occasion, he contrived to secrete,
and when alone, he used it in enlarging a small
hole in the floor. It was just behind the trap-door,
by which, when thrown open, it was entirely hidden
from view, and thus escaped discovery. Through
this hole Burns made known his situation to some
slaves in a room below, and at once enlisted their
sympathies. The intercourse thus established was

afterward regularly maintained. To avoid detection, it was carried on only at dead of night; then, throwing himself prostrate upon the floor and applying his mouth to the aperture, Burns whiled away hour after hour in converse with his more fortunate fellow bondmen. He filled their eager and wondering ears with the story of his escape from bondage, his free and happy life at the North, his capture, and the mighty effort that it cost the Government to restore him to Virginia. He was their Columbus, telling them of the land, to them unknown, which he had visited; inspiring them with longings to follow in his track; and warning them, out of his own experience, of the perils to be avoided. On their part, they communicated to him such information as their less restricted condition had enabled them to obtain. Conversation was not the only advantage that he derived from this quarter. His new friends furnished him with tobacco and matches, so that, during the long night watches, he was able to solace himself by smoking.

After a while, he found a friend in the family of Lumpkin. The wife of this man was a "yellow woman" whom he had married as much from necessity as from choice, the white women of the South refusing to connect themselves with professed slave traders. This woman manifested her compassion for Burns by giving him a testament and a hymn-book. Upon most slaves these gifts would have been thrown away; fortunately for Burns, he had learned to read, and the books proved a very treasure. Besides the yellow wife, Lumpkin had a black concubine, and she also manifested a friendly spirit toward the prisoner. The house of Lumpkin was separated from the jail only by the yard, and from one of the upper windows the girl contrived to hold conversations with Anthony, whose apartment was directly opposite. Her compassion, it is not unlikely, changed into a warmer feeling; she was discovered one day by her lord and master; what he overheard roused his jealousy, and he took effectual means to break off the intercourse.

In the search of Anthony's person at the common jail, some things had escaped discovery. He had concealed between the parts of his clothing a little money, some writing paper, and a pen, and these he still retained. Ink only was wanting, and this, through the aid of his prison friends, he also secured. Thus furnished, he wrote several letters to his friends at a distance; in all there were six, two of which were addressed to persons in Boston. To secure their transmission to the post-office, he adopted the following method : The letter was fastened to a piece of brick dug from the wall; then watching at his window until he saw some negro passing outside the jail fence, he contrived by signs to attract his attention and throw to him the letter. The passer-by was in all probability an entire stranger, as well as a person unable to read, yet Burns trusted, not unreasonably, that his wishes would be rightly interpreted, and that his

17

letters would reach the post-office. No answers were expected in return, none would have reached him had they been written. The postmaster at the South, albeit an officer of the Federal Government, is not the less an obsequious servant of the slaveholder. If a letter addressed to a slave bears a southern post-mark, it is delivered to its claimant without question; but when the post-mark indicates a northern origin, the postmaster withholds it from the claimant, inquires his master's name, and then deposits it in the latter's box. If the letter is found to be objectionable, it is destroyed and nothing is said about it; if otherwise, the master reads to his slave such portions as he sees fit. One of the letters written by Burns was addressed to Col. Suttle, giving an account of his illness. Suttle immediately wrote to Brent upon the subject, and the confounded agent hastened to the jail for an explanation. Burns frankly told him of the manner in which he had despatched his letters to the post-office, and enjoyed not a little his visitor's astonishment at the revelation. The consequence was that Brent deprived him of his pen in the vain hope of putting an end to his letter-writing.

After lying in the jail four months, his imprisonment came to an end. It had been determined to sell him, and the occurrence of a fair in Richmond presented a favorable opportunity. Accordingly, his manacles were knocked off, his person was put in decent trim, and he was led forth to the auction room. A large crowd of persons was already as-

sembled. As he stepped upon the auction block,
he saw standing a few feet off, Col. Suttle, who at
once saluted him with the old, " How d'ye do,
'Tony?" This was the first interview between
master and slave that had taken place since Col.
Suttle left the revenue cutter for New York. Presently the auctioneer ordered him to face round,
and Col. Suttle was lost to his view. While thus
standing, the voice of Col. Suttle fell upon his ear,
saying to the auctioneer, " Don't sell him to a
Yankee trader." Glancing his eyes one side,
Burns caught another sight of his master; it
proved to be the last, as the words addressed to
the auctioneer were the last words that Burns
ever heard him speak. Vindictiveness toward the
offending slave, and bad faith toward the North,
marked the spirit in which Col. Suttle finally
severed the relation between himself and Anthony
Burns.

The elevation of Burns upon the block, in full
view, was the signal for an explosion of wrathful
feeling. Angry speeches were made about him
and he was personally insulted. The violence of
one encouraged that of another, and the tumult,
momently increasing, threatened to burst over all
bounds. For awhile, Burns stood in imminent
peril of his life. With much ado, the more rational
portion succeeded at length in calming the fury of
the rest, and the auction was allowed to proceed.
It was commenced by a bid of ten dollars from
the auctioneer. No one offered more, and for a

long time the sale hung on that bid. At length the auctioneer bethought him to mention that Burns was a preacher. This caused the bidding to move on, and, in the end, he was knocked down for $905, to David McDaniel, of Rocky Mount, North Carolina. Four months before, Col. Suttle had refused to accept twelve hundred dollars from the northern friends of Burns. Meanwhile he had lost the interest on that amount, had lost the services of his slave for that length of time, and for that length of time had been compelled to pay his board. The whole transaction, while it revealed the true character of Col. Suttle, furnished an impressive illustration of slaveholding thrift.

The sale was no sooner over, than Burns was hurried back to his old quarters in the jail. Thither his new owner shortly followed, and in a personal interview made known his wishes.

"I understand," said he to Burns, "that you are a preacher. Now, I have a great many other slaves, and you are not to preach to them. If you want to preach to anybody, preach to me."

He demanded of his new slave a pledge that he would conform to this requirement. Anthony refused to give it, but at the same time promised to be a faithful servant so long as he should remain with McDaniel, provided he was well used. Otherwise, he distinctly avowed his determination to run away on the first opportunity. This frankness pleased the slaveholder. His countenance relaxed, and telling Anthony that he liked his pluck, he declared that he had no fears of his running away. The interview resulted in establishing between them a good understanding that was never afterward seriously interrupted.

To avoid the hazards of a mob, McDaniel found it prudent to remove his obnoxious slave from the city by night. About three o'clock in the morning, the two stole forth from the jail and made their way to the railroad station. Taking passage in the next train, they were soon set down at Rocky Mount in the northeastern part of North Carolina. McDaniel's plantation lay at a distance of three or four miles, and thither they were conveyed in a private vehicle.

17*

CHAPTER XI.

THE RANSOMED FREEDMAN.

At Rocky Mount, Burns entered on the last stage of his life as a slave. He was there introduced to new scenes and subjected to new influences. His new master was a different person from Col. Suttle. He possessed a more marked character, and a far greater capacity for business. In person he was short but stout, with a large head, and a countenance indicative of firmness, courage, and decision. He had an iron will that was made the law for all within his sphere; but he could appreciate and honor manly qualities in others. While his sharp, stern style of address would cause most persons to shrink away, he was not displeased when any one had the courage to stand up and confront him with manly self-assertion. Though he practically manifested but little respect for the decalogue, he made it a point of honor to fulfill his engagements.

The business of Mr. McDaniel was that of a planter, slave-trader, and horse-dealer combined. He possessed an extensive plantation, which was chiefly devoted to the culture of cotton. For the management of this, he kept constantly in his ser-

(198)

vice a large body of slaves. The number of these was constantly changing. Sometimes there would be as many as one hundred and fifty on the plantation at once; sometimes not more than seventy-five. This fluctuation was owing to the purchase and sale that was constantly going on. The plantation was made subservient to the slave-trading. The slaves were always for sale, but, while waiting for customers, they were kept at work instead of lying idle in barracoons. When a customer offered, he was accommodated, and when the stock ran low, it was replenished.

The domestic relations of McDaniel were in keeping with his character and pursuits. His wife stood in great fear of him. She presided over his household, but neither inspired nor enjoyed his respect. The tender bond of children was also wanting between them. He kept a harem of black girls, and took no pains to conceal the fact from his wife. By some of these, children were born to him, but, true to his instincts as a slave-trader, he made merchandise of them and their mothers without compunction.

The post which was assigned to Burns by his new owner was that of coachman and stable-keeper. As a horse-dealer, McDaniel kept on hand a large stock of horses and mules, often as many as a hundred at once. The stables of these animals were placed under the charge of Burns, and he held the keys. But he was required to groom and serve only the carriage-horses and his master's filly; the rest of the animals were cared for by other slaves. Whenever his mistress was inclined to take an airing, or visit a neighbor, or ride to church, it devolved on him to drive her carriage. The whole service which he was thus required to perform was light and pleasant.

His personal accommodations were better than they had ever been before. Instead of being compelled to turn in with the slaves at their quarters, he had a lodging assigned him in an office, and partook of his meals in the master's house. He was allowed to obtain what he wanted at a store of which McDaniel was the proprietor. His religious privileges were less attended to. Twice only, during his four months' servitude, was he able to attend church on Sunday. Whenever he drove his mistress to church, which was not often, he was required to wait with the horses outside while she worshipped within. It has been seen that he refused to give his owner a pledge to refrain from preaching among the slaves. In this he was governed by a sense of duty. He had been regularly invested with the office of a slave-preacher, and it was his purpose to exercise it as he had opportunity. Accordingly, during his period of service with McDaniel, he succeeded in holding, at various times, six or eight preaching-meetings among the slaves on the plantation. Once he was discovered, but his master chose to take no notice of the offence. The manliness and general good disposition of Burns so won his regard, that he tolerated in him what he would have punished in another. On his part, Burns was deeply impressed by the liberal treatment of his master, and he subsequently declared that he could not, in conscience, have run away so long as it continued. It was a matter of special favor that he was not placed under the control of an overseer, but was held accountable only to his master. The office in which he lodged was shared with him by one of the overseers. This equality of their condition, or some other cause, impelled the overseer to pick a quarrel with Burns, and he carried it so far as once to draw a pistol upon him. Burns made complaint of the assault to McDaniel, from whom, in consequence, the overseer received a stern rebuke.

His relations with his mistress were less agreeable. In striving to please his master he displeased her. McDaniel had given him express instructions to pay no heed to her commands, if they conflicted with his own. Once, in his absence, she demanded of Burns his master's favorite saddle-horse for her own use. On his refusing, she took the animal and rode off. In the mean time, McDaniel returned, and, finding what had happened, gave his wife a severe reprimand and justified Burns.

Buried thus in the obscurities of slavery, Anthony remained for some months wholly lost to the knowledge of his northern friends. All efforts on their part to discover his retreat were fruitless. On the other hand, several letters which he had

written to them, and which would have imparted
the desired information, never reached their destination; probably they were never suffered to leave
the post-office in which he had deposited them.
At length, an accident revealed the place of his
abode. He had one day driven his mistress in her
carriage to the house of a neighbor, and, while sitting on the box, was pointed out to the family as
the slave whose case had excited such commotion
throughout the country. It chanced that a young
lady residing in the family heard the statement, and
by her it was repeated in a letter to her sister in
Massachusetts. By the latter the story was related in a social circle where the Rev. G. S. Stockwell, one of the clergymen of the place, happened
to be present. This person immediately addressed
a letter to Anthony's owner, inquiring if the slave
could be purchased. An answer was promptly
returned that he might be purchased for thirteen
hundred dollars. This information was communicated to Mr. Grimes, accompanied by a declaration
that it was the purpose of the clergyman to free
Anthony, and also by an inquiry as to the amount
of money which could be obtained in Boston for
the purpose. Mr. Grimes returned answer, after
making some inquiry of former subscribers, that
he thought one half of the sum might be obtained
in Boston. It was accordingly agreed that the
labor of obtaining the whole amount should be
equally divided between the two. A fortnight
after, however, Mr. Stockwell wrote Mr. Grimes

that he should try to secure seventy-five dollars for expenses, and urged Mr. Grimes to get the thirteen hundred dollars as soon as possible. Thus the whole responsibility of the affair was once more thrown upon Mr. Grimes.

It was not by accident that this man became a chief actor in the transactions narrated in this volume. His life had been consecrated to this sort of service, and he was now only continuing what he had long before begun. An outline of his previous history will be a proper introduction to the account of his further, and, as the event proved, successful, efforts for the liberation of Anthony Burns.

Born in Virginia in the midst of slavery, though of free parents, Leonard A. Grimes was yet slightly connected by blood with the oppressed race. Left an orphan at the age of ten years, he was placed in the charge of an uncle, but the new home did not prove to be a pleasant one. Being taken to his native place on a visit, he refused again to become an inmate of his uncle's family, and soon after went to reside in Washington. There he passed several years of his life, first in the capacity of a butcher's boy standing in the public market, and subsequently as an apothecary's clerk. At length he attracted the favorable regards of a slaveholder, into whose service he was persuaded to enter upon hire. He became the confidential agent of his employer, and a deserved favorite with all the members of his family. But neither gratitude for kindness, nor love of gain, could induce him to become a participator in the great wrong of slavery. Offered the post of overseer, which had become vacant, with a salary tenfold his pay, he did not hesitate to refuse it. Far enough from any taint of abolitionism at the time, a sort of unconscious abhorrence of slavery preserved him from the contamination.

The business of his employer often led him on long journeys through the southern States, when he was accompanied by young Grimes. On one of these occasions, as they were riding through a patch of forest in North Carolina, the screams of a woman pierced their ears. On gaining the open country, they beheld near the road-side a female slave naked to the waist, and by her side an overseer lashing her with his heavy thong. The dark surface of her back was already barred with broad red stripes, while the blood poured down her limbs and stood in little pools at her feet. The employer of Grimes was a humane man, though a slaveholder, and his blood boiled at the sight. Drawing a pistol, and riding up to the miscreant, he ordered him to desist or he would instantly shoot him through. The overseer sullenly replied that he was punishing the woman because she had come late to her work. " My baby was dying, and will be dead before I see it again," interposed the wretched mother by way of excuse. She was roughly ordered off to her work, and the slaveholder, still keeping a vigilant eye on the movements of the overseer, rode on his way.

This scene wrought a revolution in young Grimes. It was his first vision of the bloody horrors of slavery, and it made him the uncompromising and life-long foe of that atrocious institution. Until now he had never been led to reflect upon the true character of the institution of slavery in the midst of which he had been born and nurtured. The sight of the bleeding mother, in her double agony of separation from her dying child and of ignominious torture in her own person, produced a shock that threw wide open his eyes and forever dispelled his indifference. His physical system became disordered; "I grew sick," said he, "and felt a sensation as of water running off my bowels. I longed for permission from my employer to shoot the man dead."

Returning home, he soon had an opportunity to put in practice the new purpose of his heart. A female slave on a neighboring plantation had received from an overseer thirty lashes for attending a religious meeting, and had fled to the estate of Grimes's employer, one of whose slaves was her husband. The case was brought to the knowledge of Grimes, and by him she was soon put upon the road to Canada, whither her husband shortly followed her. This was his induction into an office in which he afterward made full proof of his ministry to those in bondage

Leaving his employer's service, he purchased,

18

with his carefully saved earnings, one or two carriages and horses, and set himself up in business as a hackman in the city of Washington. Prosperity attended him; carriage was added to carriage, and horse to horse, until he became one of the foremost in his line of business. Thus he went on for twelve years, and while his coaches were in constant requisition by the gentry of the capital, they were not seldom placed at the service of the fugitive from southern bondage. The slaveholder oftentimes pressed the seat that perhaps the day before had been occupied by the flying slave.

At length a crisis came. The wife and seven children of a free negro were about to be sold by their master to a southern slave trader, and sent to the far south. In his distress, the husband and father applied to the man who kept coaches and horses for the use of fugitive slaves. Mr. Grimes was not backward to listen to his cry. Under the cover of a single night's darkness, he penetrated thirty miles into Virginia, brought off the whole imperilled family, and while the owner's posse, in hot pursuit, were, five hours later, blindly groping after them in Washington, they passed in disguise almost before the hunters' faces on their way to the northern land of freedom. Three months after, Mr. Grimes was arrested, taken into Virginia, and tried for his offence. The jury found him guilty, not however in accordance with the evidence, which totally failed, but to save their own lives and the life of the prisoner from an infuriated mob that had surrounded the Court House during the whole trial, and had only been kept from invading the hall of justice and committing murder by the presence of a strong military force. Sentenced to hard labor for two years in the State prison at Richmond, he there, through the instrumentality of a godly slave, (temporarily placed there for safe keeping and not for crime), experienced that great spiritual change which makes all things new for the soul. Like Paul, he straightway preached Jesus, and within two months, five of the prisoners were made partakers with him of that freedom wherewith Christ maketh free. Returning to Washington at the expiration of his sentence, he prudently abandoned the now, for him, suspicious business of a hackman, and contented himself with the humbler employment of jobbing about the city with a "furniture car." Having been admitted into the visible church, he ere long felt a divine impulse to preach the gospel. After due examination by a council of which the President of Columbian College was moderator, he received license to preach. Without abandoning the business of jobbing, he exercised his gift of preaching as opportunity offered. But the atmosphere of Washington did not permit him to breathe freely, and he sought a home in a free State.

Coming to Boston, he found there many fugitive slaves, wandering as sheep without a shepherd. He gathered them into a large upper room and preached to them the gospel. They entreated him to remain and minister to them. He consented; attendants on his ministry multiplied, and soon a church of fugitive slaves was organized in the metropolis of New England. The upper room became too strait for them, and, through the zeal and energy of Mr. Grimes, a commodious and handsome structure began to rise from its foundations. Then came the fugitive slave act, pouring ruin on this thriving exotic from the south. The church was arrested midway toward its completion, and the members were scattered in wild dismay. More than forty fled to Canada. One of their number, Shadrach, was seized, but, more fortunate than the hapless Sims, who had no fellowship with them, he succeeded in making good his escape. When the first fury of the storm had blown over, Mr. Grimes set himself with redoubled energy to repair the wastes that had been made. He collected money from the charitable, and purchased the members of his church out of slavery that they might return without fear to the fold. He made friends among the rich, who advanced funds for the completion of his church. At length it was finished, and, as if for an omen of good, was dedicated on the first day when Burns stood for trial before Mr. Commissioner Loring.[1] In

---

[1] The church is a neat and commodious brick structure, two stories in height, and handsomely finished in the interior. It will seat five or six hundred people. The whole cost, including the land, was $13,000, of which, through the exertions of Mr. Grimes, $10,000 have already been paid. The engraving is an accurate representation of its appearance.

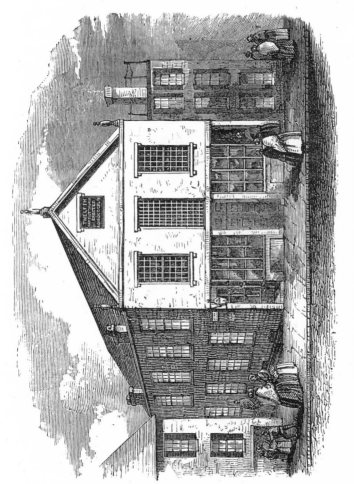

CHURCH OF THE FUGITIVE SLAVES IN BOSTON

now devoting himself to the ransom of this last victim of the oppressor, he but added one more to the long list of acts that had given character to his whole life.

Finding the business on his hands, Mr. Grimes proceeded to prompt and energetic action. His first care was to have Mr. McDaniel informed that his terms were accepted; and an appointment was made to meet him with Anthony in Baltimore on the twenty-seventh of February, and there complete the negotiation. He then laid the subject before the Baptist clergy of Boston at their weekly meeting. Most of them entered warmly into his plan and engaged to take up collections in their several churches. The same course was pursued toward the clergy of other denominations with various degrees of success. From these sources, about three hundred dollars were obtained. Three of the old subscribers redeemed their pledges by the payment of one hundred dollars each; and smaller sums were obtained from other persons of less means. When the day for his departure for Baltimore arrived, Mr. Grimes had succeeded in collecting only six hundred and seventy-six dollars. At the last moment, it seemed likely that the plan would fall through. The whole sum must be taken to Baltimore, and Mr. Grimes had no means of his own to make good the deficiency. The time had been fixed, McDaniel would be on the spot, and finding no purchaser, would depart in a state of irritation and sell Anthony to go south, as he

18*

had already threatened in one of his letters. In this emergency, the friendly cashier of a Boston bank stepped in to Mr. Grimes's relief. He received the amount already collected, accepted the note of Mr. Grimes for the balance, and placed in his hands a cheque on a Baltimore bank for thirteen hundred dollars. Thus furnished, Mr. Grimes took his departure for the Monumental city. It had been agreed that he should be accompanied by Mr. Stockwell, but, through some misunderstanding, the latter failed to appear at the place and time appointed. Mr. Grimes proceeded alone, and at eleven o'clock on the twenty-seventh of February arrived at Barnum's Hotel in Baltimore.

Meanwhile, McDaniel had broken the subject to Anthony. On receiving the first letter from Mr. Stockwell, he asked the slave if he had been writing letters to the North. Anthony evaded the question. McDaniel then informed him of Mr. Stockwell's proposition to purchase him, and inquired if he would like to have his freedom. Burns hesitated to answer, fearing that he should be entrapped. He asked permission to look at the letter, which was readily granted. Finding that McDaniel had truthfully represented the matter, he then frankly avowed his desire to be free and go to the North. Nothing more passed until the letter was received which announced the acceptance of McDaniel's terms and fixed the day of meeting in Baltimore. Soon after, Anthony drove his master to the railroad station for the purpose of taking the train to Richmond.

On alighting, Mr. McDaniel paced the ground to and fro, absorbed in thought. At length he addressed Anthony:

" I am going to tell you a secret; you must communicate it to no one, not even to my wife; what do you think it is?" continued he, after a pause.

Anthony professed that he could not imagine, unless it was that some news had come from the North. McDaniel then informed him of the happy prospect before him, and, directing him to be in readiness to depart for Baltimore on the following Monday, once more repeated his injunction of secrecy. It was at no small risk to himself that he was about to set at defiance the public sentiment of the South by sending Anthony back to the North.

Monday morning found master and slave on their journey northward by rail. Before they had proceeded ten miles, McDaniel's apprehensions were realized. Through the carelessness or treachery of a friend whom McDaniel had made a confidant, it became known that the obnoxious fugitive was on board. The passengers were quickly in a tumult, and it was proposed to stop the train and put the " boy " out. The conductor protested that had he known in the outset who Anthony was he would not have permitted him to enter the cars at all. The firmness of McDaniel, however, held the mob spirit in check, and Anthony was at length suffered to proceed without further molestation.

On arriving at Norfolk, they immediately went on board the steamer bound for Baltimore. Leaving Burns in the vessel, McDaniel went back into the city to transact some business. Meantime, the mischievous passengers of the railroad train had circulated the news of Anthony's presence. The waspish little city was at once thrown into angry commotion and forthwith swarmed in a body on board the vessel. There, on returning soon after, McDaniel found his man Anthony surrounded by the chivalry of Norfolk, and half dead through fear of their threatened violence. Sending him below deck, McDaniel faced the excited throng. They demanded that he should forego his purpose, and offered him fifteen hundred dollars for his slave. He declined the offer. They then pressed him to name his own price. His reply was that he had agreed to take Burns to Baltimore, and he intended to keep his word if it cost him his life. They then attempted to move him by intimidation, but this only roused his spirit. For an hour and a half, with pistol in hand, he kept them at bay. At last, he was allowed to depart on giving assurance that if the Massachusetts purchasers failed to keep their appointment, he would immediately return and dispose of Burns at Norfolk.

Without further molestation they pursued their way to Baltimore, and arrived at Barnum's Hotel about two hours after Mr. Grimes. The latter was absent at the moment, but, returning shortly after, was immediately ushered into the private apartment where the two travellers were secluded. Anthony greeted him with a face all radiant with happiness, and then, turning to his owner, exclaimed, " I told you it must be Mr. Grimes." In explanation of this, McDaniel said that Burns had constantly maintained, notwithstanding the correspondence had been conducted by Mr. Stockwell, that Mr. Grimes would be found at the bottom of the efforts for his liberation.

Negotiations were at once commenced. Mr. Grimes produced his cheque on the Baltimore bank, but the cautious slave trader required the cash. Accordingly, Mr. Grimes went to the bank to get the cheque cashed, but found to his annoyance that, by a rule of the institution, some citizen of Baltimore was required to certify that he was the person named in the cheque. He was unknown to a single individual in the city. From this dilemma he was relieved by the kindly aid of the landlord, Barnum. The cheque was indorsed to McDaniel, Barnum made the necessary certification in his behalf, and the cash was obtained. Before signing the bill of sale, the thrifty slave trader required an additional sum of twenty-five dollars to defray his expenses. Remonstrance was unavailing, and it was paid. The transaction being completed, Mr. Grimes pleaded with McDaniel to make Anthony a present of a hundred dollars with which to begin his new life; but the plea was met by the reply that twice that amount had already been sacrificed in keeping the engagement.

By this time a rumor of Burns's presence had got into circulation, and some feeling began to be displayed among the people in the hotel. Mr. Grimes, in consequence, decided at once to leave the city. As he and Burns passed out of the hotel, they met, upon the threshhold, Mr. Stockwell, who had that moment arrived. Finding the business completed, he turned and accompanied them back to the railway station. There they encountered another of the thousand safeguards erected by slavery, for its protection, at the expense of perpetual vexation to freemen. This was a regulation of the railroad company requiring a bond of one thousand dollars to hold the company harmless for carrying negroes. Through the friendly offices of Mr. Barnum, who signed the instrument, this obstacle was surmounted; the train then whirled off, the land of bondage was forever left behind, and that night Anthony Burns slept in Philadelphia, a free man upon free soil.

From this period he entered upon his career as a citizen of the United States, equal in the eye of the law to his former owners, and entitled to all the immunities and privileges which they could claim. But, though invested with this high title, it was practically of little or no avail to him throughout one half of the Union. It was true that the Constitution more unequivocally guarantied his protection as a freeman than his restoration as a slave; but all experience had shown it to be also true that this guaranty was for him, and such as him, worth absolutely nothing. With a solemn constitutional pledge that he should be protected in the enjoyment of all rights of citizenship while sojourning anywhere within the domain of the Union, he yet could not venture to set foot again upon the soil of his native state. Henceforth the only home for him was in the North.

On the day following his manumission he proceeded to New York, and, in a public assembly which was gathered to welcome him, narrated his story. Early in March he repaired to Boston, where preparations had been made to give him a public reception and congratulate him on the recovery of his freedom. A large meeting was held in Tremont Temple, and there, surrounded·by many clergymen, and others of note, Burns stood forth upon the platform and repeated his tale of outrage and suffering. His manly address, the sobriety of his speech, and the degree of intelligence which he manifested, took his audience by surprise and won for him increased respect. " Burns is more of a man than I had supposed," said the Rev. Mr. Kirk in his address on the occasion; " he has spoken to my heart to-night like a man. He has the true oratorical ring in him, like that of some of the Indian orators."

This meeting was followed by others of a like character in various parts of the Commonwealth. The people were eager to see the man whose enforced return to slavery had so convulsed the State. Nor did they fail to accompany the gratification of their curiosity with substantial tokens of their sympathy. It was far from Anthony's wish or intention, however, to gain a livelihood by making merchandize of his wrongs.[1] The calling to which he had devoted himself while a slave, he was more than ever bent on pursuing now that he had become a freeman. He still felt it to be his duty and desire to preach the gospel. This decision received the approval of his friends, and they took measures to promote his design. To qualify him for the sacred office, it was necessary that he should pass through a complete course of study. A lady of Boston, who held a scholarship in the Institution at Oberlin, offered to place him on that foundation. This offer was gratefully accepted, and early in the summer of 1855, he entered upon his studies in that Institution.

Soon after taking up his residence at Oberlin, he addressed a note to his old pastor in Virginia, requesting a letter of dismission and general recommendation from the church of which he had been a member while in bondage. To this request no direct answer was ever returned. But it served, apparently, to remind pastor and church of the great neglect of duty toward the institution of slavery of which they had been guilty; and they proceeded to repair that neglect by excommunicating Burns, for "disobeying both the laws of God

[1] Immediately after Burns recovered his freedom, the great showman, Barnum, addressed a letter to one of his friends offering him $500 if he would take his stand in the Museum at New York, and repeat his story to visitors for five weeks. When Burns was made to comprehend the nature of this proposal, he rejected it with indignation. "He wants to show me like a monkey!" said Burns.

and man by absconding from the service of his master and refusing to return voluntarily." Four months after, he received a copy of a newspaper containing a communication signed by the pastor and addressed to himself. It included the sentence of excommunication, and a defence of slavery drawn from the New Testament by the pastor, together with a rebuke of all christian anti-slavery men. To this communication Burns published an answer, which showed not only his ability to cope with the Virginia pastor in argument, but also his progress in a sound interpretation of the Bible.[1]

Thus by the hand of unchristian rudenesss was severed the last tie that connected Anthony Burns with the land of bondage.

[1] See Appendix K.

19

CHAPTER XII.

WHILE Burns was rehearsing the story of his great wrong in the cities and villages of Massachusetts, the Commissioner, by whose act he had suffered, was himself put on trial at the bar of the People. The part which he had played in the tragedy of June had drawn upon himself the hostile attention of large masses of his fellow-citizens, while the tragedy itself had precipitated a political revolution of which he was destined to be a conspicuous victim. A glance at the posture of affairs in the Commonwealth, during the period immediately preceding that event, will reveal more fully the causes of that revolution.

In the beginning of the year 1853, the whigs of Massachusetts recovered the control of the government which they had held for nearly a quarter of a century, but of which, for the two years previous, they had been deprived. Their new hold of power was, however, by no means secure. Their opponents, powerful in numbers and personal influence, regarded their success as an accident, and confidently looked forward to a speedy reversal of the popular decision. A Con-

vention for revising the Constitution had been
ordered; and, at the elections in the spring, the
Opposition secured a large majority of its members.   The summer saw the Convention in full
operation, and the majority, exulting in their
strength, proceeded to make the most radical
changes in the Constitution.   In the autumn, they
appealed to the people for a ratification of their
work.   It was decisively refused.   The blow was
doubly fatal, for it crushed not only the new Constitution, but also the party which had devised it.
Again the whigs returned to power, and with
vastly augmented strength.   A wise improvement
of past experience was all which they now needed
to secure them firmly in their ancient seats.   They
had lost power in the first instance by crossing
the anti-slavery sentiments of the people; they
were sure to retain and increase it by reforming
their policy on that subject.   An opportunity to
test their disposition was almost immediately presented by the proposal to repeal the Missouri
Compromise.   As the party in power, as the party
to whom had been entrusted the privilege of uttering authoritatively the voice of Massachusetts in
such a crisis, it was their duty to have led off in
an instant, energetic, and indignant rebuke of the
premeditated wrong.   But they hung back until
their defeated foes led the way, and then feebly
followed with cautiously-worded protests.   That
was not all.   Of the two Massachusetts members
of the United States Senate, Edward Everett and

Charles Sumner, the former was a representative of the whig party, and the latter a representative of their opponents. Most unfortunate for the whig party was the contrast presented by the conduct of the two in the strife about the Missouri Compromise. While Mr. Sumner extorted admiration, even from his opponents, as the gallant and courageous champion of Massachusetts, the whig Senator compelled his friends to hang their heads in shame by tamely apologizing for having presented to the Senate the noblest remonstrance ever made in behalf of the imperilled cause of human freedom.[1] Having begun by thus damaging the anti-slavery character of his party, he finished by resigning his place at a moment when the Legislature had put it out of their power, by a final adjournment, to provide a permanent successor. The prize of the vacant senatorship at once became a powerful incentive to revolution. It stimulated alike the aspiring and the patriotic among the Opposition to indefatigable efforts to replace the retiring, not to say retreating, Senator with one who would stand shoulder to shoulder with the remaining Senator. Then followed that embattled assault by the Federal Government in behalf of Virginia slavery, upon the peace, and dignity, and cherished faith of Massachusetts, the like of which had not been witnessed within her borders since the Boston Massacre of 1770. Again was a great

---

[1] Remonstrance of three thousand ministers of New England against the repeal of the Missouri Compromise.

opportunity presented to the whig party. The insulted Commonwealth demanded a demonstration
against the unpardonable outrage, and a fit demonstration could only come from the party in power.
They were the State; in their keeping was its
honor; they only could utter its voice with authority. But they did nothing; — and again they did
nothing. Then, and from that hour, the whig
party rushed swiftly downward to its ruin. A
movement in another direction concurred to hasten
the catastrophe. Some months before, a secret
political association had been organized in the
State. Its growth had been small, and, down to
the period of Burns's arrest, it continued small. But
its organization was thorough, and its machinery
the most controlling and effective ever devised. It
invited recruits, and, to all political wanderers and
malcontents, held out the alluring prospect of a
new home and new means of power. And now,
on the one hand, the discomfited and scattered members of the Opposition, and on the other, the discon-
tented portion of the party in power, together plunged
headlong into the recesses of this invisible party.
All through the summer and early autumn the
exodus from the old parties went steadily on ; as the
day of election approached, it went on with accel-
erated velocity. At length, the thirteenth of November revealed to the world the astounding result.
The whig party had vanished away. Of the sixty
thousand that had borne it into power the year
before, but twenty-seven thousand remained. In

its place had come up, eighty thousand strong, a party which at the previous election had no existence. City and country had alike yielded to their power. The great metropolitan stronghold had been stormed, and the remotest village, whether of Berkshire or Cape Cod, had been penetrated and revolutionized. Everything was theirs. Theirs was the Governor, for the first time in a decade of years by the popular vote; theirs was the entire Senate; theirs, with three or four exceptions, was the multitudinous House of Representatives. The revolution was complete and universal.

The party thus puissantly inaugurated, now turned their attention to the outrage which had so signally contributed to their success. Representing the State by a more indisputable title than any party which had ever before been entrusted with power, they proceeded to pronounce the judgment of the State upon that transaction. Two methods of procedure were possible. They might enact a general law, or they might deal with the particular actors in the tragedy, if any were found to be properly within their purview. Both methods were adopted, but with the latter only is this history concerned.

Of the obnoxious actors in the tragedy of Burns, no one was within reach of the power of the State but the Commissioner, Edward Greeley Loring. This person was one of that class of men who never, except by accident, appear on the page of history. A lawyer of moderate abilities, he had passed the middle period of life without having made any figure at the bar, and was content to solicit from his professional brethren that class of business technically called office-practice. Unambitious and reserved, he had never mingled with the people nor courted their favor in the political arena; and, until his obnoxious conduct elevated him into notice, he was probably unknown to the greater part of his fellow-citizens. But he had powerful friends, through whose influence, direct or indirect, his fortunes were essentially advanced. Among them was that family already mentioned in this history as distinguished for its devotion to the fugitive slave law, one of whose members then occupied a seat on the bench of the Supreme Court of the United States. Connected with this family by the ties of blood, Mr. Loring was in a position, on the one hand, to claim the benefit of their influence for himself, and on the other, to be infected by their peculiar views on the subject of fugitive slaves. But however this may be, he succeeded in gaining places of public trust and emolument. In 1839, he was appointed a Commissioner of the United States for taking bail and affidavits, to which duty was added, by the statute of 1850, that of sending back fugitives into slavery. In 1847, he was appointed Judge of Probate for the county of Suffolk. This office he exercised to the general satisfaction of the county. In 1854, he was chosen by the Corporation of Harvard College, a Lecturer in the Law School of that institution; but, though he at once entered on the discharge of his duties, the choice awaited the sanction of the Overseers. All of these places he held at the time of the rendition of Burns, and onward. With the office in which he had offended, the state authorities had no power to interfere, and in those over which they had control, he had done nothing amiss. Notwithstanding, it was resolved to manifest their sense of his offensive conduct in the former, by depriving him of the latter.

The willing disposition of the Legislature to proceed against Mr. Loring was sustained and stimulated by the action of the people. Hardly had the two Houses been organized, when from all quarters petitions for his removal from the office of Judge of Probate began to pour in. Every day witnessed fresh accessions to the number, and in no long time it had swelled to more than twelve thousand. On the other hand, but more tardily, remonstrances against the removal were presented. The whole number of these was less than fifteen hundred. Between remonstrants and petitioners there was a marked contrast. All of the former were men, and generally were men belonging to the circle in which Mr. Loring more immediately moved. But the petitioners were from among the broad mass of the people; and many of them were women, who, as being a class of persons deeply interested in the character of Probate Judges, very properly exercised their right of petition on this occasion.

Roused by the signs of impending danger, Mr. Loring at last himself presented to the Legislature a remonstrance against his removal. This paper was clumsily constructed and its argument was obscurely set forth. Reduced to a logical form it seemed to be this: That Mr. Loring ought not to be removed from the office of Judge of Probate; first, because his action in the case of Burns had been only that of a good citizen and a sworn magistrate both of Massachusetts and of the United States; second, because that action was not incompatible with his duty as a Judge of Probate. The fugitive slave law had found him holding the office of a Commissioner, and had imposed upon him the additional duty of sending back fugitive slaves. That law was an amelioration of the old law of 1793. It had been pronounced by the Supreme Court of Massachusetts to be constitutional; and he had been required by the people of Massachusetts to swear as Judge of Probate to support all constitutional laws. Thus, although he had sent Anthony Burns back into slavery, he had done it humanely, constitutionally, and in obedience to his oath. Nor was the act inconsistent with the faithful discharge of his Probate functions. The office of United States Commissioner had been held by state magistrates, and, therefore, might be held by a Judge of Probate. He had received the appointment of a Probate Judge while holding the office of Commissioner, and no objection had been made from any authoritative quarter against his continuing to discharge all its duties. Nor, when by the act of 1850, the duty of returning fugitives to slavery had been added to his other duties as Commissioner, had he received any notice from the state authorities that the two offices were thereby rendered incompatible. Long custom, and expressive silence twice repeated, thus sanctioned the position that a Judge of Probate might properly act as a United States Commissioner, and, so acting, might without blame send back a fugitive into slavery.

The conclusion of the remonstrance was in no suppliant tone. " I claim as facts," said the remonstrant, " that the extradition of fugitives from service or labor is within the provisions of the Constitution of the United States ; that the U. S. act of 1850 was and is the law of the land; and, by the Supreme Judicial Court of this commonwealth, obligatory on all its magistrates and people; that action under the said act was lawful and not prohibited by any State law to the judicial officers of the State, and was in conformity with the official oath of all officers of the State to support the Constitution of the United States. And I respectfully submit to your honorable bodies, that when your petitioners ask you to punish a judicial officer for an act not prohibited by any statute of Massachusetts, but lawful under those statutes, and imposed by that law of the land which is the law of Massachusetts, they ask of you an abuse of power for which the legislative history of Massachusetts furnishes no precedent."

The petitions and remonstrances were referred to the Joint Committee on Federal Relations, consisting of two Senators and five Representatives. Before this Committee had taken any action a heavy blow from another quarter fell upon the Commissioner. It has already been stated that his appointment as Lecturer in the Law School of Harvard College awaited the sanction of the Board of Overseers. This body was composed of the Governor, the Lieutenant-Governor, the President of the Senate, the Speaker of the House, the Secretary of the Board of Education, the President and Treasurer of Harvard College, and thirty other persons elected for a term of years. Its meetings were usually held only during the session of the Legislature. Whatever action had been taken by the Corporation during the legislative recess was then presented for confirmation. At the first meeting this year, held on the twenty-sixth of January, the President of the College laid before the Board Mr. Loring's appointment. The Board took time to deliberate. At the end of three weeks a second meeting was held, when the question again came up. A ballot was taken, and it was found that two thirds had voted against confirming the appointment. Among those who thus put the seal of their condemnation on the Commissioner, were the Governor and Lieutenant-Governor of the Commonwealth, and two ex-Gov-

ernors— a whig and a democrat— both of whom
had enjoyed in a rare degree the favor of their
respective parties.[1] No debate was held, and no
reasons were assigned by the majority for their adverse action. There was no need, for no one
doubted that the Board had taken this method to
express their disapprobation of Mr. Loring's conduct as Commissioner. By this stroke he was deprived of an honorable office and a salary of fifteen hundred dollars.

Four days after, the Committee held their first
meeting to consider the question of his removal
from the office of Judge of Probate. The grave
character of the proposed step invested their proceedings with unwonted interest. Only thrice
since the adoption of the Constitution had a Massachusetts Judge been removed from office by the
method of Address; never had one been removed
for such a cause. Ample powers had been granted
to the Committee. Witnesses were to be examined and arguments to be heard; the proceedings
assumed the breadth and importance of a great
public trial. To accommodate the people, the
committee-room was abandoned, and the sessions
were held in the Hall of the Representatives.
Long before the appointed hour, the spacious
apartment was filled to its utmost capacity; crowds
besieged the doors outside, and hundreds more,
unable to get within ear-shot, reluctantly went
away. This extraordinary exhibition of popular

[1] Governor Briggs and Governor Boutwell.

interest was repeated at the second hearing, a week later, and was not diminished when, on the sixth of March, the final hearing was had.

Testimony was taken respecting the Commissioner's conduct, both in and out of the court-room, during the trial of Burns. But the time was chiefly consumed by arguments from various persons in favor of the removal. Among these, the most distinguished were Wendell Phillips, Theodore Parker, and the historian, Richard Hildreth. They spoke for the twelve thousand petitioners, and for the vast multitude beside, whom those petitioners represented. Much of what was in the public mind, much of what had appeared in the public journals, was now brought to bear upon the Committee with all the force which rare eloquence and keen dialectic skill could exert.

The reasons urged in favor of the removal were various, but they were all reducible into two classes; those which had respect to the character and conduct of Mr. Loring, and those which had respect to the character and conduct of Massachusetts. The Commissioner, it was said, had not conducted the examination of Burns fairly and uprightly. He had pushed it on with indecent haste. He had manifested a purpose to send back the prisoner without giving him a chance for defence. A stickler for law, he yet had wrested the law to the prejudice of the prisoner's rights. He had received the admissions of the prisoner so far as they told

20

against him, and excluded them so far as they told in his favor. He had suffered the worst part of the community to be admitted into his court-room, and the better part to be debarred therefrom. He had refused to secure for the prisoner's counsel free access to his court. He had prejudged the prisoner's cause. Before the examination was fairly begun, he had on two different occasions more than hinted that Burns would have to be sent back to Virginia.[1] He had also, in effect, prejudged the cause by preparing a bill of sale of the prisoner. All these things were so many disclosures of character; they showed Mr. Loring's unfitness for the office of a Massachusetts Judge. He ought, therefore, to be removed.

But there was another view. Some, not stopping to inquire whether as Commissioner he had acted well or ill, held it to be the head and front of his offence that he had acted at all. He should not have sat in judgment on the case. He should not have issued his warrant. He should have resigned his place as Commissioner if he could not otherwise have honorably retained it. Whatever might be his private views, as Judge of Probate he was bound to keep himself free from the contamination of slave-catching. Moreover, he had violated the spirit of the Constitution, and especially of the Bill of Rights. By that charter, Massachusetts

[1] See letters of Charles Grafton and Edward Avery to the Committee on Federal Relations, printed in House Document, No. 93.

magistrates were required to "observe justice, piety, and moderation;" to countenance the principles of humanity and benevolence.   But slave-catching was opposed to all these.   Nor was that all; he had violated an express statute of the Commonwealth. By the law of 1843, all Massachusetts officers and magistrates were forbidden to assist in the business of returning fugitive slaves, and the terms of this law were held to include Judges of Probate. Finally, whatever view might be taken of the past, Mr. Loring had manifested a purpose to continue in the business of a slave-catching Commissioner; he had even insisted that it was a solemn duty which he could not evade.   If, therefore, he were longer suffered to retain his judicial office, Massachusetts would proclaim to the world that her Judges of Probate might properly, and without offence, act a chief part in sending back into perpetual slavery persons as much entitled to compassion as widows and orphans.

These reasons were of a punitive character; they had respect mainly to Mr. Loring.   But the removal was placed upon higher and broader ground.   It was necessary to vindicate the character and to enforce the behest of the Commonwealth. From the earliest days, Massachusetts had taken up a position on the subject of slavery in advance of every other nation in Christendom.   During the period of her colonial independence, she had adopted the Mosaic code for her guide, and, while not daring to prohibit what God had permitted,

had yet reduced slavery to its minimum of evil.[1]
During the subsequent period of her provincial
vassalage under royal governors, the power of the
Crown was interposed to arrest her tendencies
toward the entire abolition of the system, and

[1] A small volume has recently been presented to the Massachusetts
Historical Society, entitled, "Abstract of the Lawes of New England
as they are now Established," and printed in London in 1641. By
the code there given, manstealing was punished with death. In the
same year the following statute was enacted : "It is ordered by this
Court and the authority thereof, That there shall never be any bond
slavery, villenege, or captivity amongst us, unless it be lawful cap-
tives taken in just warrs, as willingly sell themselves, or are sold to
us, and such shall have the liberties and Christian usage which the
law of God established in Israel concerning such persons, doth
morally require, provided this exempts none from servitude who
shall be judged thereto by authority." [i. e. as a punishment for
crime.] I have traced this statute in the edition of the Laws of
1660, and in that of 1672. There is no doubt that it continued in
force till the abrogation of the Charter in 1684. Among the "liberties and Christian usage" secured by other enactments, were these :
A servant flying from the tyranny and cruelty of his master to the
house of a freeman, was to be protected and sustained there till due
order was taken for his relief. No servant was to be put off to
another person for above a year, neither in the lifetime of his master
nor after his death, by an executor, except by the authority of
Court, or of two Assistants. [An "Assistant" in those days exercised
the functions both of a Senator and of a member of the Governor's
Council.] A servant whose tooth was smitten out by his master,
was to go free from service and have such further recompense as
the Court should adjudge. (Mass. Laws, 1660.) There was also
this important statute in which the bondman is placed on an equality
with the freeman : "Every man, whether inhabitant or foreigner,
free or not free, shall have libertie to come into any publique court,
councel, or towne meeting, and either by speech or writing to move
any lawful, seasonable, or material question, or to present any necessary motion, complaint, petition, bill, or information, whereof that
meeting hath proper cognizance, so it be done in proper time, due
order, and respective manner."

she was compelled to endure what she was unable
to remedy.[1]   But from the hour when she recovered

[1] There is abundant evidence that the people of Massachusetts
were, during the provincial period, opposed to slavery, and would
fain have got rid of it, but were prevented by their governors.   In
1701, only nine years after the colony was transformed into a royal
province, the representatives of Boston were requested by that town
to take measures to put a stop to negro slavery.   The preamble of
an act passed in 1703, declares that "great charge and incon-
veniences have arisen to divers towns and places by the releasing
and setting at liberty mulatto and negro slaves."   In 1705, heavy
duties were imposed by the General Court on imported slaves, with
a view to discourage the business.   In 1712, was passed "an act to
prohibit the importation or bringing into this Province [Massa-
chusetts] any Indian servants or slaves;" and one of the reasons
assigned for the measure is, that such importation "is a discourage-
ment to the importation of white Christian servants."   About the
year 1716, Samuel Sewall, Chief Justice of the Province, published
a pamphlet in condemnation of slavery.   In 1767, an attempt was
made to pass a law "to prevent the unnatural and unwarrantable
custom of enslaving mankind and the importation of slaves into
the province."   In 1769 one James, a negro, brought a suit in the
county of Suffolk, against one Lechmere, to recover his freedom,
and was successful.   Other suits were brought in other counties, and
they were uniformly decided in favor of the slaves.   The ground of
these decisions was said to be, that all persons in the Province were
by the charter as free as the king's subjects in England, and there
slavery was not recognized by law.   In 1774, a bill to prevent the
importation of slaves passed the two Houses, but Gov. Hutchinson
refused to sign it *because his instructions from the king forbade*.   Gov.
Gage refused his signature to a similar bill for the same reason.
In 1777, during the revolutionary war, a prize ship with a cargo of
slaves was brought into Salem, and the slaves were advertised to be
sold; but the Legislature then sitting in that town interposed, prevented the sale, and ordered the slaves to be set at liberty.   For
most of these facts, see a learned and instructive article on slavery,
in the 41st volume of the North American Review, from the pen of
the Hon. Emory Washburn, late Governor of the Commonwealth.

20*

her ancient independence, slavery was forever
banished from her domain.[1] Becoming a member

---

[1] Slavery was abolished in Massachusetts by virtue of the clause
in her Constitution which declares that "all men are born free and
equal." The great honor of having made that clause a part of the
Constitution belongs to JOHN LOWELL. This distinguished man
was born at Newburyport in 1743, and was graduated at Harvard
College in 1760. He commenced the practice of the law in his native town, but in 1776 removed to Boston. He soon after became a
representative in the General Court, and also a member of the Convention which framed the Constitution of the State. In 1781 he
was chosen a member of the Continental Congress. In 1782 he
was appointed Judge of the Admiralty Court of Appeals. On the
establishment of the Federal Government in 1789, he was appointed
by Washington, District Judge of the United States for Massachusetts. This office he held till 1801, when, upon a reörganization of
the courts, he was made Chief Justice of the new Circuit Court for
the eastern district. His death took place in 1802. "He was,"
says Cushing in his history of Newburyport, "eminent for his judgment, integrity, and eloquence as an advocate and legislator; for
his impartiality, acuteness, and decision as a judge; and for his zeal
in the cause of scientific and other useful institutions."

Mr. Lowell was the bosom friend of the elder Adams, with whom
he was associated on the sub-committee for drafting the plan of the
Constitution. Respecting his agency in procuring the adoption of
the clause which abolished slavery in Massachusetts, I am happy in
being able to present the testimony of his son, now venerable for
years and virtues, the Rev. Charles Lowell, D. D., of Cambridge.
In a recent note addressed to me, he says : "My father introduced
into the Bill of Rights the clause by which slavery was abolished in
Massachusetts. You will find, by referring to the Proceedings of
the Convention for framing the Constitution of our State, and to
Elliot's N. E. Biographical Dictionary, that he was a member of
the Convention and of the Committee for drafting the plan, &c.,
and that he suggested and urged on the Committee the introduction
of the clause, taken from the Declaration of Independence a little
varied, which virtually put an end to slavery here, as our courts decided, as the one from which it was taken ought to have put an end

of the Federal Union, she also became subject to the fugitive slave law of 1793. But she never ceased to detest it, and when, exactly half a century after, a fit occasion was furnished by a decision of the United States Supreme Court, she hastened to place upon her statute-book an act expressive of her detestation and of her ancient and unalterable convictions. In this attitude the fugitive slave law of 1850 met and confronted her. It soon became manifest that as the new law was far more stringent and oppressive than the old, so it was to be enforced with far greater activity. Almost immediately after its enactment, a negro was arrested, under its provisions, within the borders of Massachusetts. Fortunately for himself and for the peace of the Commonwealth, he escaped from custody before the law had taken its course. Soon, another was arrested and sent back into bondage at the South, there, as it turned out, to suffer imprisonment, scourging, and death. In no long time after, occurred the arrest and extradition of Anthony Burns. It seemed that the soil of Massachusetts was about to become a permanent hunting-ground

to slavery in the United States. This he repeatedly and fully stated to his family and friends. . . . . . . In regard to the clause in the Bill of Rights, my father advocated its adoption in the Convention, and, when it was adopted, exclaimed: '*Now there is no longer slavery in Massachusetts; it is abolished, and I will render my services as a lawyer gratis to any slave sueing for his freedom, if it is withheld from him,*' or words to that effect." Mr. Lowell's view of the effect which the clause would have, was speedily confirmed by a decision of the Supreme Court. See Appendix L.

for Southern slave-catchers.   What was she to do?
She could not follow the example of South Carolina; she could not nullify a law of Congress;
she could not arm her citizens and bid them resist
by force the execution of the law.   Nor did she
need so to do; for she held in reserve a great constitutional resource.   By the terms of the Federal
Constitution, she had reserved to herself all the
rights and attributes of sovereignty not expressly
granted to the Federal Government.   She had
thus reserved to herself, as an individual in the
family of States, the right of private judgment upon
the constitutionality of federal laws.   She had reserved the right of influencing her citizens, within
the sphere of voluntary action, against assisting to
execute an obnoxious law.   She had reserved the
right to say upon what conditions her citizens
should enjoy the honors and emoluments of offices
within her own gift, upon what conditions these
should be forfeited.   And if she chose to make
the voluntary aiding to execute the fugitive slave
law one of those conditions, such was her sovereign
right.   Nor was it more a sovereign, a constitutional, than it was a moral right.   The citizen of
Massachusetts, though he owed allegiance to the
United States, owed a higher allegiance to his own
State.   For it was she, and not the former, that
chiefly provided for his welfare.   At her hand he
obtained his elective franchise, his schools, his
roads, his police.   He touched the State at almost
all points, the Federal Government at scarcely

more than one. If, therefore, a conflict of views arose between the two, the State rightfully claimed that her sentiments should be respected, rather than those of the more distant, less protective Power.

The conduct of Mr. Loring furnished an occasion for the practical illustration of this doctrine. Massachusetts had passed resolves expressive of her disapprobation of the fugitive slave law. She had passed an act to discountenance its execution within her territory. But neither acts nor resolves had proved sufficient. An example was needed to enforce the precept. The removal of Mr. Loring would teach her citizens more impressively than a whole statute-book of resolves, that, if they desired to enjoy her favor, they must conform to her views respecting the execution of the fugitive slave law.

The Commissioner was formally notified to appear before the Committee, if he chose, and make answer to what might be said against him. In a brief note he declined the privilege, and contented himself with referring the Committee to his remonstrance as containing all that he had to say. An unexpected champion, however, volunteered to maintain his cause. At the third and last hearing, Richard H. Dana, Jr., presented himself before the Committee, and asked to be heard in behalf of the remonstrants. No man in the whole Commonwealth occupied at that moment so commanding a position for influencing the Committee, the Legislature, and the public in favor of the Commissioner. As the defender of Burns, he had won the applause and gratitude of those who were now pursuing the Commissioner. He had been in the best position to witness the Commissioner's demeanor during the examination. He was a most competent judge of his official conduct, and was not likely to judge it more favorably than facts would warrant. He had freely condemned the Commissioner's decision; and he protested that he now appeared before the Committee, not for Mr. Loring's sake, but for the sake of the principle involved.

That principle was the independence of the Judiciary. Its preservation, Mr. Dana argued, was a thing of the highest moment to the welfare of the State and of every citizen. But, if Judge Loring were to be removed by the method proposed, and for the reason alleged, it would receive a shock of the most serious character. True, the Constitution gave to Government the power of removal by Address; but it was a power exceedingly liable to abuse, and this removal would be a most signal instance of its abuse. For it was not pretended that Mr. Loring had been guilty of any official misconduct; he was to be deprived of an office in which it was admitted he had borne himself well, because in another capacity he had offended the popular will. If by such an example the Judges of Massachusetts were taught to square their conduct by the views of the party in power, their independence would soon vanish away.

To this argument the answer was short and con-

clusive.   The independence of the Judiciary can
never be threatened by a removal, it was said,
unless the removal is made on account of some
judicial act.   But it was not proposed to remove
Judge Loring for any judicial act; his removal,
therefore, could not possibly influence the judicial
conduct of other judges.   Their conduct in another
respect it would indeed powerfully influence; for,
with such a beacon in view, no Judge of Probate
would afterward venture to lend his aid in executing
the fugitive slave law.   But this result was precisely what was aimed at, and it was entirely consistent with the independence of the Judiciary.

Having concluded his argument on this point,
Mr. Dana assumed the character of a witness, and,
moved either by compassion or love of justice,
delivered a generous testimony in the Commissioner's behalf.   His conduct toward the prisoner Mr.
Dana regarded as considerate and humane.   He
had encouraged Burns to resolve upon making a
defence.   He had postponed the examination from
Thursday to Saturday, and again from Saturday
to Monday, in order that counsel for the defence
might have time to make preparation.   He had
commanded the Marshal, contrary to that officer's
inclinations, to admit Mr. Phillips and others to
the prisoner's cell for the purpose of arranging for
a defence.   He had zealously co-operated with
others in the attempts to purchase the prisoner's
freedom ; and had even gone so far as to draw up
an order, in view of the contemplated purchase,

for his release from custody. These were facts which Mr. Dana thought should have their just weight in determining the culpability of the Commissioner.

But all arguments and representations, even when proceeding from such an influential source, failed of producing their intended effect. On the twenty-second of March, the Committee made their report. It was not a model state paper, but its substance was weighty and close to the point. It sharply dissected the Commissioner's remonstrance, largely vindicated the right of the Legislature to proceed by the sovereign method of Address, and recapitulated, under four heads, the objections against the Commissioner. It concluded with recommending that an Address should be presented to the Governor requesting him to remove Mr. Loring from his judicial office. This report was signed by four of the Committee. Of the remaining three members, two presented a statement of reasons for not signing the report of the majority, and the third presented a minority report. Both agreed with the majority in their premises, but dissented from their conclusion.

The question of adopting the report came up in the House on the twenty-seventh of March. But before any action was taken, the reports were recommitted, at the instance of Mr. Dana, for the purpose of hearing further testimony on the question whether the Commissioner had prejudged the case of Burns. On the third of April, a meeting of the Committee was held and much testimony was taken.   Its effect was simply to strengthen the case against the Commissioner.   On the fourth, the Committee reported back to the House the original report slightly altered, and it was made the special assignment for the tenth.   During the forenoon and afternoon of that and the two following days, it was warmly debated.   Various expedients were devised to avert the impending blow, but none of them availed.   On the fourteenth, the House resolved, by a vote of two hundred and six against one hundred and eleven, to send an Address to the Governor.

The action of the Senate was even more decisive.   On the twenty-seventh of the same month that body, after mature deliberation, concurred with the House by a vote of twenty-seven against eleven.

Within a few days after, a Committee of both Houses proceeded to the Council Chamber and presented the Address to the Governor.   It was in these words :

" The two branches of the Legislature, in General Court assembled, respectfully request that your Excellency would be pleased, by and with the advice of the Council, to remove Edward Greely Loring from the office of Judge of Probate for the county of Suffolk."

The Governor of the Commonwealth at this time was Henry Joseph Gardner.   Like his predecessor in office, John Hancock, of illustrious memory, he was a Boston merchant; but there the parallel ended. Mr. Gardner had never, like him, rendered any service to the State which could possibly mark him out as a fit person to be crowned with the honors of the chief magistracy. Prior to his elevation, he had been placed by his fellow-citizens of Boston in various situations favorable for winning distinction — in municipal office, in the Legislature, in the Constitutional Convention — but in none of them had he risen above the level of respectable mediocrity. In the Constitutional Convention, which embraced the chief men of all parties in the state, his position was among the followers and not among the leaders; throughout its deliberations he acted no conspicuous part, nor did he leave the impress of his mind on any measure, whether of those that were adopted or of those that were rejected. The dissolution of that body left him in the position of a private citizen. While thus situated, a sudden freak of fortune elevated him to the chief place of honor in the Commonwealth. Early in the autumn following the extradition of Burns, a convention of the secret party already mentioned, assembled in secret to nominate a candidate for Governor. After a fierce contest among the partisans of several candidates whose names had been made familiar to the public, the choice of the convention, to the surprise of every one, fell upon Mr. Gardner, whose name had not even been mentioned. In the canvass which followed, he displayed qualities as a political tactician of which his previous career had given no promise. He adopted a line of policy, the audacity of which confounded his foes and excited the admiration of his friends. His master-stroke was a proclamation by letter of his abhor-rence of the fugitive slave law. To this public assurance, were added private assurances of a still stronger character. Thus pledged on the great grievance which Massachusetts had to redress, Mr. Gardner was borne triumphantly into power.

The removal of Judge Loring became the first and chief test of his fidelity to his pledges. Had op-portunity been presented for him to act on the case immediately after his election, there was no reason to doubt that he would have promptly made the removal. But in the interval of six months which elapsed, a change came over the complexion of public affairs that raised doubts about the course he would take. Opinion was divided. Those who desired the removal were confident that he would comply with their wishes, for he had privately in-formed some of their number that he longed for an opportunity to do the deed. Others, who drew their conclusions from different premises, predicted that he would court the favor of Virginia and risk that of Massachusetts.

Speculation was speedily put to rest. On the tenth of May, Governor Gardner transmitted a message to the Legislature declining to comply with the prayer of their Address.

Thus ended the trial of the Commissioner. Through the intervention of the Governor he was

suffered still to enjoy the emoluments of his office.
But no Governor could deprive the judgment of
the Legislature of its moral power. In the archives
of the State is laid up, for perpetual remembrance, a
record declaring it to be the will of Massachusetts,
that under no plea of duty to the Federal Government shall her Judges of Probate be suffered to
compromise her character by sending back fugitives
into slavery.

LIBERTY and LAW are both precious to the
People of Massachusetts. But Law is precious as
the guardian of Liberty and in nowise as her oppressor. When Law turned against Liberty in the
epoch of 1776, the People rose and put down Law.
But after Liberty had been reinstated in her right-
ful supremacy, their next care was to re-establish
Law also. The lesson contained in this History
points to the same result. It represents Law in
the attitude of striking Liberty with the military
arm, and the People aroused and angered by the
assault. Their passion rose not then to the height
of overwhelming Law, but it rose to the height of
warning against a repetition of the tragic act.
The remedy of 1776 will be their reluctant last
resort, but they are pledged by the Declaration to
its use when every other fails. And meanwhile,
they will be swift to punish, as the enemies of both,
those who array Law against Liberty. The Crest
of their escutcheon is not an unmeaning symbol.

APPENDIX.

APPENDIX A.

United States of America, Massachusetts District, ss.

To the Marshal of our District of Massachusetts, or to either of his Deputies, Greeting:

IN the name of the President of the United States of America, you are hereby commanded forthwith to apprehend Anthony Burns, a negro man, alleged now to be in your District, charged with being a fugitive from labor, and with having escaped from service in the State of Virginia, if he may be found in your precinct, and have him forthwith before me, Edward G. Loring, one of the Commissioners of the Circuit Court of the United States for the said District, then and there to answer to the complaint of Charles F. Suttle, of Alexandria in the said State of Virginia, merchant, alleging, under oath, that the said Anthony Burns, on the twenty-fourth day of March last, did, and for a long time prior thereto had owed service and labor to him, the said Suttle, in the State of Virginia, under the laws thereof; and that, while held to service there by said Suttle, the said Burns escaped from the said State of Virginia into the said State of Massachusetts; and that said Burns still owes service and labor to said Suttle, in the said State of Virginia, and praying that said Burns may be restored to him, said Suttle, in said State of Virginia, and that such further proceedings may then and there be had in the premises as are by law in such cases provided. Hereof fail not, and make due return of this writ, with your doings thereto, before me.

Witness my hand and seal, of Boston aforesaid, this twenty-fourth day of May, in the year one thousand eight hundred and fifty-four.

EDW. G. LORING, Commissioner.

United States of America, Boston, Massachusetts District, ss.
May 25, 1854.

Pursuant herewith, I have arrested the within named Anthony Burns, and now have him before the Commissioner within named, for examination.

WATSON FREEMAN, United States Marshal.

APPENDIX B.

Commonwealth of Massachusetts, Suffolk, ss.

To the Sheriff of our County of Suffolk, or his Deputy, or either of the Coroners thereof, Greeting:

WE command you that, justly and without delay, you cause to be replevied Anthony Burns, of Boston, in our said county, laborer, who (as it is said) is taken and detained at Boston, within our said county, by the duress of Charles F. Suttle, of Alexandria, in the State of Virginia, trader, that he, the said Burns, may appear at our Court of Common Pleas next to be holden at Boston, within and for our said County of Suffolk, on the first Tuesday of July next, then and there in our said Court to demand right and justice against the said Suttle for the duress and imprisonment aforesaid, and to prosecute his replevin as the law directs. Provided the said Anthony Burns shall, before his deliverance, give bond to the said Charles F. Suttle in such sum as you shall consider reasonable, and with two sureties at the least, having sufficient within your county, with condition to appear at our said Court to prosecute his replevin against the said Suttle, and to have his body there ready to be re-delivered if thereto ordered by the Court, and to pay all such damages and costs as shall be then and there awarded against him. Then, and not otherwise, are you to deliver him. And if the said Anthony

(249)

Burns be by you delivered at any day before the sitting of our said Court, you are to summon the said Suttle, by serving him with an attested copy of this writ, that he may appear at our said Court to answer to the said Anthony Burns.

Witness, DANIEL WELLS, Esquire, at Boston, the second day of June,[1] in the year of our Lord one thousand eight hundred and fifty-four.

JOSEPH WILLARD, Clerk.

BOND.

KNOW all men by these presents, that we, Anthony Burns, of Boston, in the County of Suffolk and Commonwealth of Massachusetts, laborer, as principal, and Francis Jackson, Timothy Gilbert, Wendell Phillips, and Samuel E. Sewall, all of said Boston, as sureties, are holden and stand firmly bound and obliged unto Charles F. Suttle, of Alexandria, in the State of Virginia, trader, in the full and just sum of five thousand dollars, to be paid unto the said Charles F. Suttle, his executors, administrators, or assigns: to which payment, well and truly to be made, we bind ourselves, our heirs, executors, and administrators, jointly and severally, firmly by these presents: Sealed with our seals. — Dated the second day of June, in the year of our Lord one thousand eight hundred and fifty-four.

The condition of this obligation is such that whereas the said Burns has this day sued out a writ of personal

---

[1] In the original, the words "thirty-first" day of "May" were first written, and afterwards erased. The writ was in fact made on Wednesday, the 31st of May, in the expectation that the decision would be pronounced on that day, and the date was altered to make it conform to the day on which it was actually pronounced.

replevin against said Suttle, returnable before the Court of Common Pleas next to be holden at said Boston, within and for said County of Suffolk, on the first Tuesday of July next —

Now if the said Burns shall appear at the said Court and prosecute his said replevin against the said Charles F. Suttle, and have his, the said Burns's, body there ready to be re-delivered if thereto ordered by the Court; and shall pay all such damages and costs as shall be then and there awarded against him — then this obligation shall be void, otherwise shall remain in force.

Signed, sealed, and delivered in presence of }	ANTONY BURNS, [Seal.] By W. PHILLIPS.
LYSANDER SPOONER, Witness to F. J., T. G., and S. E. S.	WENDELL PHILLIPS. [Seal.] TIMOTHY GILBERT. [Seal.]
CHAS. G. DAVIS, To W. P. & A. BURNS	FRANCIS JACKSON. [Seal.] S. E. SEWALL. [Seal.]

APPENDIX C.

" IN ALEXANDRIA CIRCUIT COURT, May 16, 1854. On the application of Charles F. Suttle, who this day appeared in Court and made satisfactory proof to the Court that Anthony Burns was held to service and labor by him, the said Suttle, in the State of Virginia, and service and labor are due to him, said Suttle, from the said Anthony, and that the said Anthony has escaped from the State aforesaid, and that the said service and labor are due him, the said Suttle, the master of the said Anthony; and having further proved to the satisfaction of the Court that the said Anthony is a man of dark complexion, about six feet high, with a scar on one of his cheeks, and also a scar on the back of his right hand, and about twenty-three or four years of age, — it is therefore ordered, in pursuance of an act of Congress, entitled ' An Act to amend and supplementary to the Act entitled " An Act respecting fugitives from justice, and persons escaping from their masters," ' approved Feb. 12, 1793, that the matter so prayed and set forth be entered on the record of this Court."

State of Virginia, County of Alexandria, ss.

" I, Franklin L. Burkett, Clerk of the Circuit Court of Alexandria county, in the State aforesaid, do hereby certify that the foregoing is a true transcript from the records of said Court.

"In testimony whereof, I hereto subscribe my name, and annex the seal of said Court, this 13th day of May, 1854, and in the 78th year of the Commonwealth.

[L. S.] F. L. BURKETT, *Clerk of Alexandria C. C.*"

" State of Virginia, County of Alexandria, ss.

" I, John W. Tyler, presiding Judge of the Circuit Court of Alexandria county, in the State of Virginia, do certify that Franklin L. Burkett, whose name is affixed to the preceding certificate as clerk of the said Court, is clerk thereof, and his said attestation is in due form.

" Given under my hand this 18th day of May, 1854.

"JOHN W. TYLER."

22

APPENDIX D.

FRIDAY, June 2, 1854.

MR. COMMISSIONER LORING came in at 9 o'clock, and, the parties being all present, pronounced the following

DECISION.

The question submitted to my decision is, whether I shall award to the claimant, Charles F. Suttle, a certificate, authorizing him to take and carry to Virginia the respondent, Anthony Burns, whom he claims as owing him service and labor. The kind of service which he sets up is that of a slave.

The respondent's counsel have objected to the constitutionality of the act of 1850, under which these proceedings are held, and to my right to act in the premises, on several grounds.

[The Commissioner then stated the points of objection and overruled them successively, and declared his opinion to be that, upon the precedents, he was bound to hold the statute constitutional in all the points affecting this case. We omit his decision on these points, as being of less immediate interest.]

The facts to be proved by the claimant are three :

1. That Anthony Burns was his slave by the law of Virginia.

(254)

2. That Anthony Burns escaped from slavery in Virginia.

3. That the prisoner is the Anthony Burns in question.

To prove the first point, the claimant introduces one witness, Mr. William Brent, of Virginia. Mr. Brent's testimony shows that Burns has stood in the relation of a slave to Col. Suttle from his boyhood. It also shows that, at the time of the alleged escape, Col. Suttle had leased Burns to one Millspaugh of Richmond, and that Burns was then, and had for some time been, in the custody and under the control of Millspaugh, and that he escaped, if at all, from the custody and service of Millspaugh. It is objected by the defendant's counsel, that this evidence shows that Col. Suttle is not entitled to the certificate. This raises, certainly, a serious question. By the law of Virginia, slaves are chattels, and the lessee of the chattel, being in possession, has the sole and exclusive right, against the general owner himself, to the possession and control of the chattel during the lease. The constitutionality of this statute is sustained on the ground that the decision in these proceedings affects merely the possession and temporary control of the party claimed, and does not affect the general property or title. If it were otherwise, it would constitute a suit at law, and a trial by jury would be necessary. It would seem, therefore, quite clear that upon the claimant's own theory, Mr. Millspaugh, and not he, is the person entitled to claim this certificate. If Mr. Millspaugh and Col. Suttle were to interplead before me, each claiming the certificate, I cannot doubt that I should be obliged to grant it to the former.

To prove the second point, viz.; the escape, the claimant also offers the evidence of Mr. Brent. Mr. Brent says only that Burns was in Richmond up to the 24th day of March, and was then and ever since "missing." He does not say that he went away without the leave of Mr. Millspaugh, who alone had the right to control his movements, and how or why he was missing. To explain the act of Burns, they offer evidence of his conversation with Col. Suttle, on the night of his arrest. In this conversation he says that he did not escape ; but that, being on board a vessel at work, he was tired and fell asleep, and was brought off by accident. Now this story may not be true, but it is put in by the claimant, and it is the very evidence tending to explain the act of Burns, and the claimant is bound by it. Therefore, the claimant's evidence not only fails to show an escape, but shows affirmatively that there was no escape. To entitle the claimant to his certificate, there must be, both by the Constitution and the statute, an *escape*. It is of no consequence how or why the slave came into a free state, — whether by accident or mistake, or by a superior power; unless he escaped by his own voluntary act, against the will of his master, the *casus fœderis* does not arise. (Sims' case, 7 Cush. 298.)

On the oral evidence, then, the claimant must fail on the second requirement of the statute, even if the point as to the lease were not sustained.

But the claimant puts into the case a transcript of a record made out *ex-parte*, in Virginia, in pursuance of the 10th section of the act of 1850. This act declares that this record " shall be held and taken to be full and conclusive evidence of the fact of escape, and that the service or labor of the person escaping is due to the party in such record mentioned." The record sets forth that Anthony Burns does owe service and labor to Col. Suttle by a law of Virginia, and that he escaped from such service and labor in Virginia. If, then, this record is to be received, and to have its full statutory effect, the title and escape are established, and the only question open to me is that of identity. But I should be slow to believe that any statute of this land was intended to make an *ex-parte* record conclusive against the proof actually made by the party who offers it, on a trial in presence of both parties.

Here is a trial, with witnesses on the stand, in presence of both parties, and the claimant's own proof shows him not entitled to prevail. Can it be that he may fall back upon proof offered at an *ex-parte* hearing, previously and elsewhere, and contradict and control his own proof here, and compel the Court to decide against the evidence? The defendant's counsel contend that by offering proof of the title and escape, other than the record, the claimant proceeds under the 6th section, and not the 10th, and is not entitled to use the record, the two sections providing for separate and distinct proceedings; also that the conclusiveness of the record cannot apply to the claimant's own proof, but only prohibits the defendant from controverting the record by proof. They also object to the instrument on the ground that it is not a record, but only a recital that there is a record which is not produced, and because it does not describe the party with "convenient certainty," as required by the statute, inasmuch as it does not say whether he is a white, a negro, an Indian, or a mulatto, but only that he is "dark-complexioned." If on any one of these grounds of objection the record is not received, or not allowed to have conclusive effect, the claimant must fail, because no escape has been proved, to say nothing of the objection as to the lease.

22*

Without deciding, at present, whether the record is to be received or not, I will pass to the question of identity.

The testimony of the claimant is from a single witness, and he standing in circumstances which would necessarily bias the fairest mind — but other imputation than this has not been offered against him, and from anything that has appeared before me cannot be. His means of knowledge are personal, direct, and qualify him to testify confidently, and he has done so.

The testimony on the part of the respondent is from many witnesses whose integrity is admitted, and to whom no imputation of bias can be attached by the evidence in the case, and whose means of knowledge are personal and direct, but, in my opinion, less full and complete than that of Mr. Brent. Then, between the testimony of the claimant and respondent, there is a conflict, complete and irreconcilable. The question of identity on such a conflict of testimony is not unprecedented nor uncommon in judicial proceedings, and the trial of Dr. Webster furnishes a memorable instance of it.

The question now is, whether there is other evidence in this case which will determine this conflict. In every case of disputed identity, there is one person always whose knowledge is perfect and positive, and whose evidence is not within the reach of error, and that is the person whose identity is questioned, and such evidence is offered in this case. The evidence is of the conversation which took place between Burns and the claimant on the night of the arrest.

It may be conceded that this evidence, if received and allowed its full weight, would establish the identity of the prisoner with the Anthony Burns named in the record, beyond a reasonable doubt. The conversation took place very shortly after the arrest of Burns, at the time he first discovered that he was claimed as a slave, and while he was in custody. The only person examined as to his state of mind, a witness for the claimant, says that at first Burns appeared intimidated, but latterly had been entirely composed. Of course this state of intimidation applies to the time of the conversation, which was at the first moment he knew he was held as a slave; and I remember that the next morning I thought him in such a state as to require me to allow him an adjournment, in order to make up his mind what course he would pursue. It is said that the language of Col. Suttle to him, ' I make you no promises and no threats — I make no compromises with you,' may be considered as intimidating in its character, or at least as intimating to the prisoner that his treatment hereafter would be according to his conduct there; and I am requested to rule out this evidence, on the ground that the admissions of an alleged slave to his master, while in custody during a trial for his freedom, are not legal evidence for the claimant, and on the further ground that, if not objectionable on general rules, there is evidence here of actual duress and influence. Another objection is, that the conversation put in by the claimant is entire, and that if any part of it is received, the whole must be received. His conversation, taken at the worst for the respondent, asserts that he is the party named in the record, and was the slave of the claimant, but shows that he did not escape. It is an inflexible rule of law, founded in justice, that the whole of an admission must be taken together. If, therefore, I am to receive this conversation, while it would satisfy me of the identity, it would negative the escape. But the claimant says the record is conclusive on the point of escape. If so, I must reject a portion of this conversation, because it conflicts with the record, and if I reject a part on such grounds, by the claimant's act, must I not reject the whole? If so, the identity is not proved. The claimant's case is in this dilemma. If the record is received and is conclusive, it seems to me that I must reject the entire conversation, because I cannot take the part that convicts him if I must reject the part that acquits him, and the claimant fails because the identity is left in doubt. If the record is rejected, the entire conversation goes in, the identity is proved, but the escape is negatived. Therefore, whether the record is received or rejected, the claimant must fail.

Let me restate the conclusions to which I am led, on the several points. I think myself bound by the precedents to hold the statute constitutional, and to hold that I have jurisdiction in the premises. It is the inclination of my belief that this record, if otherwise sufficient, cannot be admissible as conclusive on the Court against the positive proof of the claimant himself, and that, without the aid of the conclusiveness of the record, the claimant has not proved an escape, or a right of possession in himself. On the point of identity, even if the title and escape were proved, there is a reasonable doubt on the evidence of the witnesses, and the burden of proof is on the claimant to establish the identity beyond all reasonable doubt. If the admissions of Burns were received and allowed full weight, it would remove this reasonable doubt. To say nothing of the objections to the competency of these admissions on general principles, or under the circumstances of this case, I am not willing to receive that part of a conversation which convicts a man, if I am obliged, by the act of the other party, to reject that part which acquits him. If, therefore, the record is received, the entire conversation goes out, and the identity is not proved. If the record is rejected, the entire conversation goes in and the identity is proved, but the title and escape are not proved. On any of these grounds I am prepared to place my decision. This result may be owing to the accidents and mistakes which sometimes attend legal testimony, and arise in the vicissitudes and complications of novel proceedings at law. But I am bound to know only the evidence legally before me. The certificate is refused and the prisoner must be discharged.

APPENDIX E.

THE COMMISSIONER'S CERTIFICATE.

United States of America, Massachusetts District, ss.

WHEREAS, Charles F. Suttle, of Alexandria, in the State of Virginia, merchant, hath produced and exhibited to me the transcript of the record of the Circuit Court of the County of Alexandria, in the State of Virginia, authenticated by the attestation of the clerk, and of the said Courts, by which it appears, that on the tenth day of May last the said Suttle appeared to said Court, and made satisfactory proof to the same, that one Anthony Burns was held to service and labor by him, the said Suttle, in the said State of Virginia; and that the said Anthony escaped from the State of Virginia aforesaid; and that this said service and labor are still due to him, the said Suttle, the master of the said Anthony; and further proved to the satisfaction of the said Court, that the said Anthony is a man of dark complexion, about six feet high, with a scar on one of his cheeks, and also a scar on the back of his right hand, and about twenty-three or four years of age; and whereas, it hath also been proved before me, on the oath of a credible witness, that the said Anthony Burns, a colored man, now in the custody of Watson Freeman, Esq., Marshal of the United States, for the District of Massachusetts aforesaid, on a warrant issued by me for his apprehension, is the same Anthony Burns mentioned and described in the aforesaid transcript of a record, and therein

(262)

certified as owing service and labor to the said Charles F. Suttle, the claimant of the said Burns is authorized to re-move him, the said Burns, from the State of Massachusetts back to the State of Virginia, pursuant to the act of Con-gress passed on the 18th of September, A. D. 1850, entitled "An act to amend, and supplementary to, 'an act respecting fugitives from justice and persons escaping from the service of their masters,' approved February 12th, one thousand seven hundred and ninety-three."

Given under my hand and seal at Boston, on this second day of June, in the year one thousand eight hundred and fifty-four.

(Signed) EDWARD G. LORING, [Seal.]

One of the Commissioners appointed by the Circuit Court of the United States, for the First Circuit and District of Massachusetts, to take the bail and affidavits in civil causes.

"I have reason to believe and apprehend that said fugi-tive will be rescued from me before he can be taken beyond the limits of this State in which he has been arrested; and I therefore request the officer who made the arrest, to wit, Watson Freeman, Esq., United States Mar-shal for the said District of Massachusetts, to remove the said fugitive to said Alexandria, and there to deliver him to me."

[Extract from Suttle's affidavit before a U. S. Commissioner.]

APPENDIX F.

BOSTON, May 27, 1854, 5 o'clock, P. M.

To General B. F. Edmands:

SIR, — You are requested to keep two military companies on duty through the ensuing night, to preserve order in the city, by co-operating with the civil authorities, according to the spirit of the communication made to you in the morning, and until further orders.

J. V. C. SMITH, *Mayor.*

Commonwealth of Massachusetts, Suffolk, ss.,

BOSTON, May 27, 1854.

To Major General Benjamin F. Edmands, Commanding the 1st Division of Massachusetts Volunteer Militia.

{ Seal } WHEREAS it is made to appear to me, J. V. C. Smith, Mayor of the city of Boston, that there is threatened a tumult, riot, and mob of a body of men, acting together, by force, with intent to offer violence to persons and property, and by force and violence to break and resist the laws of this Commonwealth in the said County of Suffolk, and that *military force* is necessary to aid the civil authorities in suppressing the same, —

(264)

Now, therefore, I command you that you cause two companies of your command, armed and equipped, and with proper ammunition, as the laws direct, and with the necessary officers attached, to parade at their respective armories, at 10 o'clock A. M., then and there to obey such orders as shall be given them, according to law.

Hereof fail not at your peril; and have you then and there this warrant, with your doings returned thereon.

Witness my hand, and seal of the city of Boston, this 27th day of May, A. D. 1854.

J. V. C. SMITH,

Mayor of the City of Boston.

The following was afterward indorsed by the Mayor, upon the same warrant:

BOSTON, May 29th, 1854, half-past 12, P. M.

"You are requested to call into service two more companies, for the remainder of this day.

"J. V. C. SMITH, *Mayor.*"

CITY HALL, May 31, 1854.

General Edmands, — After a careful examination of the condition of the city this morning, I feel justified in saying, that one military company will be amply sufficient from this date, till further orders, to maintain order and suppress any riotous proceedings — acting in concert with the police.

At 9 o'clock this morning, therefore, you will please discharge one of the two companies on duty, under your command.   Very respectfully, &c.,

J. V. C. SMITH, *Mayor.*

23

Commonwealth of Massachusetts, Suffolk, ss.

May 31, 1854.

To Major General Edmands, Commanding the 1st Division of Massachusetts Volunteer Militia.

{ Seal. } WHEREAS it has been made to appear to me, J. V. C. Smith, Mayor of the city of Boston, that there is threatened a tumult, a riot, or a mob of a body of men acting together, by force, with intent to offer violence to persons and property, and to break and resist the laws of this Commonwealth, and that *military force* is necessary to aid the civil authorities in suppressing the same, —

Now, therefore, I command you that you cause the First Brigade, and the Divisionary Corps of Cadets, to be detailed from your command, and armed and equipped, and with proper ammunition, as the law directs, and with the necessary officers attached thereto, to parade on *Boston Common*, on Friday, the 2d day of June next, at 9 o'clock, A. M., then and there to obey such orders as may be given to you.

Hereof fail not at your peril; and have you then and there this warrant, with your doings recorded thereon.

Witness my hand, and the seal of the said city of Boston, this 31st day of May, 1854.

J. V. C. SMITH,
Mayor of the City of Boston.

Indorsed on this warrant is the following :

HEAD QUARTERS, 1st Div. M. V. M., }
BOSTON, June 1, 1854. }

I hereby certify that I have issued the orders necessary for assembling the force called for by this precept.

B. F. EDMANDS, *Maj. Gen.*

SPECIAL ORDER.

Brigadier General Samuel Andrews is hereby ordered to assemble his entire Brigade (1st Brigade M. V. M.) on the morning of the 2d June current, in uniform, and armed, equipped, and provided with ammunition effectively to carry out the object of the precept served upon me by his Honor the Mayor of Boston, a copy of which is herewith sent down. He will report himself with his brigade, at "the Parade" on Boston Common, to the Division Inspector, promptly at $8\frac{1}{2}$ o'clock A. M.

Lieut. Col. Thomas C. Amory will, in like manner, report himself with the Divisionary Corps of Cadets.

Field music only will be ordered on duty.

The hour fixed upon for the Brigade so to report, gives only half an hour for the formation of the Division line, and other necessary arrangements.

By command of

B. F. EDMANDS, *Maj. Gen.*

FRANCIS BOYD, *Div. Insp.*

CITY HALL, June 2, 1854.

General Edmands:

SIR, — The U. S. Marshal informs me, officially, that he shall be ready to move escort at precisely half-past 12 o'clock, and you will therefore govern yourself according. Please inform him when all is in readiness..

Very respectfully yours,

J. V. C. SMITH, *Mayor.*

The boat is at T Wharf.

CITY HALL, June 2d, 1854.

General Edmands:

SIR, — I herewith enclose a proclamation, addressed to the citizens of Boston, enjoining good order and obedience to the laws.

With high consideration, I have the honor to remain

Your obedient servant,

J. V. C. SMITH, *Mayor.*

APPENDIX G.

BOSTON, May 30, 1854.

To the Hon. J. V. C. Smith, Mayor of the City of Boston:

SIR, — From the indications of an armed resistance to
the laws, and the assurances of the military officers on
duty, it is manifest that the force now under the orders of
Maj. Gen. Edmands is not sufficient to preserve the peace
of the city. The Marshal has at his disposal, by order of
the President of the United States, all the U. S. troops, as
an armed posse comitatus, which can at present be drawn
to this point. He does not ask any aid to execute the
fugitive law as such. Nothing is required but the preservation of the peace of the city, and the suppression of
organized rebellion.

To effect this, we respectfully submit an opinion, that,
if bloodshed is to be prevented in the public streets, there
must be such a demonstration of a military force as will
overawe attack, and avoid an inevitable conflict between
the armed posse of the Marshal and the rioters; and earnestly request you, under the views which Maj. Gen. Edmands has communicated, or will communicate, to you, if
desired, that you will exercise the powers the law has confided to you, to place under his command such a body of
the Volunteer Militia as will ensure the peace of the city
without a conflict.

From the opinion of the military gentlemen with whom we have conferred, and the indications from all other sources of information within our reach, we beg leave to express the opinion that the entire command of General Edmands within the city will be requisite. We have no express authority to pledge the General Government to that effect, but we believe that the expenses incurred by the necessity of such a military force will be met by the President.

> Respectfully, your obedient servant,
> WATSON FREEMAN, *U. S. Marshal.*

Approved. — B. F. HALLETT, *U. S. Att'y.*

OFFICE OF THE U. S. MARSHAL AND OFFICE OF THE U. S. ATTORNEY, BOSTON, May 31, 1854.

SIR, — In reply to your note of this morning, we are authorized by the President of the United States to state that any expense incurred for the city military or otherwise, deemed necessary by the U. S. Attorney and U. S. Marshal to enforce the laws, will be paid by the United States.

We deem it necessary that, when the decision of the Commissioner is to be given, which will probably be to-morrow morning, the avenues and streets around the Court House should be cleared of the crowd, and an ample military force be on guard to preserve the peace of the city, and prevent riot or personal outrages, which are then to be anticipated, whatever may be the decision.

And we further deem it necessary that, if the Marshal with his posse is required to pass through the streets of the city, they should not be crowded upon, molested, or placed in a position of defence which may render it necessary to protect themselves by a resort to arms. And this requires the whole military and police force of the city to preserve the peace of the city, and prevent riot and assaults upon the officers of the law in the discharge of their duty.

We repeat what we have before said, that the United States officers do not desire you to execute the process under the *fugitive law* of the United States, which devolves on them alone in the discharge of their duties, but they call upon you, as the conservator of the peace of the city, to prevent the necessity of conflict between the posse of the Marshal and those who may attempt to resist them by force while in the lawful discharge of the duties required of them, whatever those duties may be. Herewith is a copy of the authority derived from the President of the United States.

Your obedient servants,

B. F. HALLETT, *U. S. Att'y.*
WATSON FREEMAN, *U. S. Marshal.*

WASHINGTON, May 31, 1854.

To B. F. Hallett, U. S. Attorney.

Incur any expense deemed necessary by the Marshal and yourself for city military, or otherwise, to insure the execution of the law.

(Signed) FRANKLIN PIERCE.

Hon. J. V. C. SMITH, Mayor of the city of Boston.

The United States Marshal requests that two companies of Light Infantry be on guard for the night, and until further orders.

WATSON FREEMAN, *U. S. Marshal.*

To the Mayor of the city of Boston, }
May 31, 1854. }

Approved. — B. F. HALLETT, *U. S. Attorney.*

The opinion of the Court will be given at 9 o'clock, Friday morning, and it is deemed that the request from the Marshal and U. S. Attorney, dated this day, for the whole military and police force of the city to preserve the peace of the city, take effect for Friday morning.

W. FREEMAN, *U. S. Marshal.*

Approved. — B. F. HALLETT, *U. S. Attorney.*

APPENDIX H.

BOSTON, May 27, 1854.

To the President, &c.

In consequence of an attack on the Court House last night for the purpose of rescuing a fugitive slave under arrest, and in which one of my own guards was killed, I have availed myself of the resources of the United States placed under my control by letters from the War and Navy Departments in 1851, and now have two companies of troops from Fort Independence stationed in the Court House. Everything is now quiet. The attack was repulsed by my own guard.

WATSON FREEMAN,
U. S. Marshal, Boston, Mass.

WASHINGTON, May 27.

To Watson Freeman, U. S. Marshal, Boston, Mass.

Your conduct is approved. The law must be executed.

FRANKLIN PIERCE.

WASHINGTON, May 30, 1854.

To Hon. B. F. Hallett, Boston, Mass.

What is the state of the case of Burns?

SIDNEY WEBSTER,
Private Sec'y to the President.

(273)

Boston, May 30, 1854.

The case is progressing, and not likely to close till Thursday. Then armed resistance is indicated. But two city companies on duty. The Marshal has all the armed posse he can muster: more will be needed to execute the extradition if ordered. Can the necessary expenses of the city military be paid if called out by the Mayor at the Marshal's request? This alone will prevent a case arising under second section of Act of 1795, when it will be too late to act.   B. F. HALLETT.

Washington, May 31, 1854.

To B. F. Hallett, U. S. Att'y.

Incur any expense deemed necessary by the Marshal and yourself, for city military or otherwise, to insure the execution of the law.   FRANKLIN PIERCE.

Boston, May 31.

To Sidney Webster.

Dispatch received. The Mayor will preserve the peace with all the military and police of the city. The force will be sufficient. Decision will be made day after to-morrow, of the case. Court adjourned.

      B. F. HALLETT.

Boston, June 2d.

To Sidney Webster.

The Commissioner has granted the certificate. Fugitive will be removed to-day. Ample military and police force to effect it peacefully. Law reigns. Col. Cooper's arrival opportune.[1]   B. F. HALLETT.

---

[1] Col. Cooper, Adjutant General of the army, had been ordered by the President, May 31st, to Boston, empowered to call out, if necessary, the two companies of U. S. troops at New York, which had been under arms for the preceding forty-eight hours.

APPENDIX I.

I. THE escort will consist of the Marshal's *posse comitatus.*

II. The line of march and the avenues leading thereto to be cleared of citizens, and the military and police guards of the city posted, before the escort moves.

III. The police guards to be posted across the side streets at those intersections of the avenues leading thereto which are nearest State street, and the military guards between the several police parties and State street.

IV. One company of Cavalry to be posted immediately below the old State House to support the clearing of streets if necessary; then to move from square to square as the escort moves down, preserving the same interval in advance of the escort. A patrol to be kept in front, observing the several cross streets, and, on their reports, detachments to be rapidly advanced to any point of danger.

V. The escort to move in the following order, viz.:

1st. Major Ridgely's Artillery Battalion, in posts.

2d. One platoon Marines.

3d. The Marshal's civil posse guarding the fugitive.

4th. Two platoons of Marines.

5th. Lt. Couch's field-piece.

6th. One platoon of Marines to bring up the rear of the escort and form a guard to the field-piece.

(275)

VI. A company of Cavalry to be drawn up across Court street and move toward the old State House as soon as the escort shall have passed that building, and take its position as a reserve to the whole force, first at State House and next in rear of the infantry moving down State street — ready to act as emergencies may require.

VII. The military and police detachments to move from the side avenues into State street as soon as the escort shall have passed the second side street below them, respectively, and gradually move down State street, so as to be within supporting distance should the escort be attacked. These detachments will march by a flank on the sidewalks so as to leave the street open to the advance of the Cavalry, when necessary.

June 2d, 1854.

APPENDIX J.

The resignation by Mr. Hayes of his office as Captain of Police, called forth numerous testimonials in approval of the act. Letters to that effect reached him from all quarters. One lies before me signed by seventy-one ladies of Maine. Another, from West Medway, contains one hundred and fifty signatures. The following was received from Senator Sumner:

"Washington, 9th June, 1854.

"My Dear Sir, — I desire to express to you my gratitude for your magnanimous example on a recent occasion. Of course you did right. To help enslave a fellow man in Boston cannot be less heinous, in the sight of God, than to do it on the coast of Congo. In resigning your office rather than do this thing, you have led the way which Public Opinion in Massachusetts will indicate to all good men.

"Believe me, my dear sir,
"Very faithfully yours,
"Charles Sumner.
"Joseph K. Hayes, Esq."

Testimonials of substantial value were also presented; a gold Watch from Plymouth, a Salver of massive silver from Boston. Both bore suitable inscriptions; that on the Salver was as follows:

24   (277)

"T O

"JOSEPH K. HAYES, ESQ.,

"EX-CAPTAIN OF THE WATCH AND POLICE OF THE CITY OF BOSTON,

" This Salver is presented by a portion of his fellow-citizens, as a Testimonial of their admiration for his conduct when called upon by the MAYOR of BOSTON to perform an act which he regarded as unworthy of a *Man*, an American, and a Christian.

" When directed to assist in the extradition of ANTHONY BURNS, the alleged Slave, he RESIGNED HIS OFFICE, in the following letter:

"' BOSTON, June 2, 1856.

"' *To his Honor the Mayor, and Aldermen of the City of Boston:*

"'Through all the excitement attendant upon the arrest and trial of the Fugitive by the U. S. Government, I have not received an order which I have conceived inconsistent with my duties as an Officer of the Police until this day, at which time I have received an order which, if performed, would implicate me in the execution of that infamous Fugitive Slave Bill. I therefore resign the office which I now hold as Captain of the Watch and Police, from this hour, 11 o'clock.'

" We are proud to claim as a fellow-citizen one who, though poor, cannot be bought, who loves his integrity better than his daily bread, and who has given such an example of what a TRUE AMERICAN CITIZEN should be.

" This conduct is a practical denial of the atheistic doctrine (the most dangerous to American Liberty because of its speciousness) that the law of the land has a higher sanction than the law of GOD, a doctrine which, if true, renders our Forefathers TRAITORS. our Revolution HIGH TREASON.

> " R. E. APTHORP,
> JAMES CARPENTER,
> FRANCIS CHILDS, } *Committee.*"
> GEO. B. EMERSON,
> H. A. EMERY,

APPENDIX K.

" In answer to my request by mail, under date July 13, 1855, for a letter of dismission in fellowship and of recommendation to another church, I have received a copy of the Front Royal Gazette, dated Nov. 8, 1855, in which I find a communication addressed to myself and signed by John Clark, as pastor of your body, covering your official action upon my request, as follows :

" THE CHURCH OF JESUS CHRIST, AT UNION, FAUQUIER CO.,
VIRGINIA.

" *To all whom it may concern :*

Whereas, Anthony Burns, a member of this church, has made application to us, by a letter to our pastor, for a letter of dismission, in fellowship, in order that he may unite with another church of the same faith and order; and whereas, it has been satisfactorily established before us, that the said Anthony Burns absconded from the service of his master, and refused to return voluntarily — thereby disobeying both the laws of God and man; although he subsequently obtained his freedom by purchase, yet we have now to consider him only as a *fugitive from labor* (as he was before his arrest and restoration to his master), have therefore

(280)

" *Resolved,* Unanimously, that he be excommunicated from the communion and fellowship of this church.

" Done by order of the church, in regular church meeting, this twentieth day of October, 1855.

" WM. W. WEST, *Clerk.*"

Thus you have excommunicated me, on the charge of " disobeying both the laws of God and men," " in absconding from the service of my master, and refusing to return voluntarily."

I admit that I left my master (so called), and refused to return ; but I deny that in this I disobeyed either the law of God, or any real *law* of men.

Look at my case. I was stolen and made a slave as soon as I was born. No man had any right to steal me. That manstealer who stole me trampled on my dearest rights. He committed an outrage on the law of God ; therefore his manstealing gave him no right in me, and laid me under no obligation to be his slave. God made me a *man* — not a *slave ;* and gave me the same right to myself that he gave the man who stole me to himself. The great wrongs he has done me, in stealing me and making me a slave, in compelling me to work for him many years without wages, and in holding me as merchandize, — these wrongs could never put me under obligation to stay with him, or to return voluntarily, when once escaped.

You charge me that, in escaping, I disobeyed God's law. No, indeed ! That law which God wrote on the table of my heart, inspiring the love of freedom, and impelling me to seek it at every hazard, I obeyed ; and, by the good hand of my God upon me, I walked out of the house of bondage.

I disobeyed no law of God revealed in the Bible. I

24*

read in Paul (1 Cor. 7 : 21), " But, if thou mayest be made free, use it rather." I read in Moses (Deut. 23 : 15, 16), " Thou shalt not deliver unto his master the servant which is escaped from his master unto thee. He shall dwell with thee, even among you in that place which he shall choose in one of thy gates, where it liketh him· best; thou shalt not oppress him." This implies my right to flee if I feel myself oppressed, and debars any man from delivering me again to my professed master.

I said I was stolen. God's Word declares, " He that stealeth a man and selleth him, or if he be found in his hand, he shall surely be put to death." (Ex. 21 : 16.) Why did you not execute God's law on the man who stole me from my mother's arms ? How is it that you trample down God's law against the *oppressor*, and wrest it to condemn me, the *innocent* and *oppressed?* Have you forgotten that the New Testament classes " manstealers " with " murderers of fathers " and " murderers of mothers," with " manslayers and whoremongers ? " (1 Tim. 1 : 9, 10.)

The advice you volunteered to send me, along with this sentence of excommunication, exhorts me, when I shall come to preach like Paul, to send every runaway home to his master, as he did Onesimus to Philemon. Yes, indeed I would, *if you would let me.* I should love to send them back *as he did,* " NOT NOW AS A SERVANT, but *above a servant;* — A BROTHER — a brother beloved — both *in the flesh* and in the Lord;" both a brother-man and a brother-Christian. Such a relation would be delightful — to be put on a level, in position, with Paul himself. " If thou count me, therefore, a *partner*, receive him *as myself.*" I would to God that every fugitive had the privilege of returning to such a condition — to the embrace of *such a Christianity* — " not now as a servant, but above a servant,"—a "partner,"—even as Paul himself was to Phile-mon!

You charge me with disobeying the *laws of men*. I utterly deny that those things which outrage all right are laws. To be real laws, they must be founded in equity.

You have thrust me out of your church fellowship. So be it. You can do no more. You cannot exclude me from heaven; you cannot hinder my daily fellowship with God.

You have used your liberty of speech freely in exhort-ing and rebuking me. You are aware that I too am now where I may think for myself, and can use great freedom of speech, too, if I please. I shall therefore be only re-turning the favor of your exhortation if I exhort you to study carefully the golden rule, which reads, "All things whatsoever ye would that men should do to you, do ye even so to them; for this is the law and the prophets." Would you like to be *stolen*, and then *sold?* and then worked without wages? and forbidden to read the Bible? and be torn from your wife and children? and then, if you were able to make yourself free, and should, as Paul said, "*use it rather*," would you think it quite right to be cast out of the church for this? If it were done, so wick-edly, would you be afraid God would indorse it? Sup-pose you were to put your soul in my soul's stead; how would *you* read the law of love?[1]

ANTHONY BURNS.

[1] In reply to a note which I addressed to Anthony, respecting this letter, he informed me that while he had some little assistance in its preparation, it was for substance his own.

APPENDIX L.

[The following account of the first slave case in Massachusetts
after the adoption of the State Constitution, was written by the Rev.
George Allen, of Worcester, and is taken from the appendix to a
discourse preached by the Rev. James Thompson, D. D., of Barre,
at the end of his ministry of fifty years in that town.]

This was the case of a negro man named Walker, belonging to this town (Barre). Quock, as Walker was
commonly called, — for slaves, having in law no fathers,
and their mothers no husbands, have themselves no sur-
names, but are called like horses and dogs, as the whims
of their masters and a degrading system may dictate, —
had been a slave of Nathaniel Jennison, a substantial
farmer of Barre, who still claimed him as a slave. The
constitution was ratified in the spring of 1780, and it was
now summer, when a long day's freedom was worth something more than a short day's bondage in winter. Haying
was at hand, and Quock was a rare hand at haying.
About this time, William Caldwell, senior,[1] a neighbor of
Jennison and of Quock, too, told the latter that he was a
free man, and offered him wages if he would bear the
heat and burden of the day on his farm, a proposal made
still more inviting by the promise of Caldwell that he
would stand between him and harm if Jennison should

[1] See Note at the end.

(284)

punish him for being free. Quock loved both liberty and the reward of his own hard toil, though he had never tasted of either; and being in other respects a man, though an African, pondered the matter, and resolved to be a freeman in Caldwell's employ rather than be a slave in Jennison's for nothing. Accordingly, on a summer's morning, having had orders the night before from Jennison to be up betimes and mow in his field, Quock was up by daybreak and soon found his way to Caldwell's meadow, with a scythe as busy and as sure as Time's. After a while, Jennison went to his field to see that all was well; but Quock was not there, nor any trace of his handiwork. Not a swarth was laid, not a flower of the field fallen. Jennison, who was a man of sense, quickly cast about him, and suspected the whereabouts of the fugitive. He at once hied over to Caldwell's farm, where, at a distance, he soon spied Quock, as busy in Caldwell's meadow as he had ever been in his own. He suddenly stopped on the brow of a hill and halloed to the new-made freeman *to go home.* But Quock was so attentive to his work, or so engrossed in contemplating the sweets of liberty, that he seemed to hear nothing from a distance. Jennison hurried down the hill, and, having come within sure hailing distance, tried the persuasion of *hard threats;* but all in vain, for Quock, encouraged by Caldwell's presence, and not forgetting the promise of a strong and resolute man to stand between him and harm, answered never a word, but kept on mowing as though nothing had happened. Jennison, baffled in his experiment, and well knowing where he was and with whom he had to do, went back more vexed than he came, resolved to bide his time, which, after lingering, at last came, though not altogether in the very shape he looked for. * * * *

How soon Jennison re-assumed his authority over Quock as his slave, I cannot say; but the first experiment I know of was *that which gave rise to the trial in the Supreme Court whose issue settled forever the question of slavery in Massachusetts ;* and it is remarkable that so few particulars are recorded of a case which excited, at the time of the occurrence, so much interest, and was followed by consequences so marked and lasting. Seventy years have elapsed since the issue was tried, and freedom triumphed. The men who witnessed it are gone; and the voices of tradition have become few and indistinct. The personal narrative already given is related on hearsay, not very recent. What follows I take from a copy of the record of court obtained several years ago, and now before me in the crabbed and uncouth dialect of ancient legal barbarity.

By the record it appears that " on the first day of May, A. D. 1781, the said Nathaniel, with his fist, and a large stick, which the said Nathaniel held in his hand, the said Quock did beat, bruise, and evilly intreat, and him, the said Quock, with force and arms, did imprison during the space of two hours." The indictment was found at the September term of the Supreme Court, 1781 ; but the trial did not take place till the April term, 1783, at which time Jennison was found guilty and sentenced to pay a fine of forty shillings, with the costs of prosecution, and ordered to stand committed till sentence be performed. The record states that Jennison pleaded *not guilty*, but does not indicate the ground of his defence, nor any opinion of the court from which it might be inferred. Both, however, are briefly stated by Dr. Belknap, in his correspondence with Judge Tucker of Virginia, in 1796, in which he says, " His (Jennison's) defence was, that the black was his slave, and that the beating, &c., was the necessary restraint and correction of the master. This was answered by citing the clause in the declaration of rights, 'all men are born free and equal.' The judges and jury were of opinion that he had no right to beat or imprison the negro." (Collections of Mass. Hist. Society, vol. IV.)

The issue of the prosecution of Jennison was virtually the decision of the highest tribunal in the State, that slavery had no legal existence in Massachusetts; and its immediate effect was to set free all who were held in bondage within her jurisdiction. It carried out, in its true idea, the unanimous resolve of the convention that formed the constitution, " that the government of Massachusetts shall be a FREE REPUBLIC." It was the first decision on this continent, if not the first in the world, which gave freedom to the collective slaves of a sovereign State, where a like servitude had been expressly or tacitly allowed. Several cases, however, had occurred in other parts of Massachusetts, of slaves sueing their masters in the inferior Courts for freedom and wages; and "the juries invariably gave their verdict in favor of liberty; " but the legal effect of such verdicts reached none but the parties immediately concerned. * * * * I have searched, both here and in Boston, where the early records of the Supreme Court were exclusively kept, for the list of the grand jury which formed the indictment, but without success. The names of the jury which tried the *Barre Slave Case*, if I may now venture to call it such, were, foreman, Jonas How, and fellows, William McFarland, Isaac Choate, Joseph Bigelow, John White, Daniel Ballard, Ebenezer Lovell, Phillips Goodridge, John Lyon, Jonathan Woodbury, Thomas White, and John Town.

NOTE. — It was not William, but John Caldwell. I have this fact from his grandson, Seth Caldwell, Esq., of Barre, who had frequently heard both his father and his grandfather relate all the circumstances. From the same source I have derived some additional particulars of interest which I will here set down.

John Caldwell was a man of property and influence, and the leading magistrate in the town. Before the Revolution, he had represented Barre in the General Court. In advising Quock of his rights as a freeman, he did no worse for his neighbor Jennison than he had done for himself; for he had already emancipated his own slave, Mercy, and not only so, but had also made provision for her comfort. Another neighbor, John Black, had emancipated his slave Dick, Mercy's husband, at the same time. Caldwell and Black then built a small house and presented to the pair, and they dwelt in it for many years afterwards, earning their own support. Not long after Quock left Jennison, the latter went over to Caldwell's farm with several men, for the purpose of removing his slave (as he still called him) by force; but Quock, backed by Caldwell, presented so bold a front, being determined to resist, even unto blood, that Jennison thought it prudent to retire, without even attempting a seizure. Quock continued with Caldwell until his freedom was legally decreed, Caldwell acting as his chief friend and adviser in carrying the case through court. He afterward married, became the possessor of a little homestead in Barre, and there continued to reside until his death, which occurred about forty years since.

Quock had a younger brother, named Prince Walker, who was also the slave of Jennison. When about seven years old, he was sold to a man in East Windsor, Ct. Prince kept the reckoning of his age until he was twenty-one, and then escaped from his master and returned to Barre. His master followed and made repeated efforts to recover him, but without success. This "fugitive slave case" occurred about two years after the passage of the Fugitive Slave Act of 1793. Slavery had previously been abolished in Connecticut, and it does not appear on what ground the reclamation was made. Prince, like his brother, married and settled in Barre, where he is still living (August, 1856), at a very advanced age. He is, perhaps, *the last survivor of the Massachusetts slaves.* — C. E. S.

APPENDIX M.

SPEECH OF THEODORE PARKER AT THE FANEUIL HALL MEETING.

[The speech which follows was phonographically reported for the Worcester Daily Spy. It should have been inserted at page 39 of this volume, but I was not made aware that such a report, or indeed that any report, was in existence, until a large part of the work had been stereotyped.]

Fellow-subjects of Virginia, — [loud cries of "no, no," and "you must take that back!"] *Fellow-citizens of Boston, then,* — ["yes, yes,"] — I come to condole with you at this second disgrace that is heaped on the city, made illustrious by *some* of those faces that were once so familiar to our eyes (alluding to the portraits of the great men of the past, which *once hung* conspicuously in Faneuil Hall, but which have been removed to obscure and out-of-the-way locations). Fellow-citizens, a deed which Virginia commands has just been done in the city of John Hancock, and the "brace of Adamses." It was done by a Boston hand. It was a Boston man who issued the warrant; it was a Boston Marshal who put it in execution; they are Boston men who are seeking to kidnap a citizen of Massachusetts, and send him into slavery for ever and ever. It is our fault that it is so. Eight years ago, a merchant of Boston "kidnapped a man on the high road between Faneuil Hall and old Quincy," at 12 o'clock — at the noon of day; and the next day mechanics of this city

25   (289)

exhibited the half-eagles that they had received for their share of the spoils, in enslaving a brother man. You called a meeting in this hall. It was as crowded as it is now. I stood side by side with my friend and former neighbor, your honorable and noble chairman to-night [loud cheers], and that man who had fought for the cause of liberty in Greece, and been imprisoned for that sacred cause in the dungeons of Poland (Dr. Samuel G. Howe), stood here and introduced to the audience that " old man eloquent," John Quincy Adams [loud cheers]. It was the last time he ever stood in Faneuil Hall. He came to defend the inalienable rights of a friendless negro slave, kidnapped in Boston. There is even no picture of JOHN QUINCY ADAMS to-night! A Suffolk grand jury could find no indictment against the Boston merchant for kidnapping that man ["shame," "shame"]. If Boston had spoken then, we should not have been here to-night. We should have had no Fugitive Slave Bill. When that bill passed, we fired a hundred guns. Don't you remember the Union meeting, held in this very hall? A man stood on this platform — he is a Judge of the Supreme Court now — and he said, "When a certain 'reverend gentleman' is indicted for perjury, I should like to ask him how he will answer the charge?" And, when that " reverend gentleman " rose, and asked, " Do you want an answer now to your question?" Faneuil Hall cried out, "No," "no," — "Throw him over!" Had Faneuil Hall spoken then on the side of truth and freedom, we should not now be the subjects of Virginia. Yes, we are the *vassals* of Virginia. It reaches its arm over the graves of our mothers, and it kidnaps men in the city of the Puritans, over the graves of Samuel Adams and John Hancock [cries of "shame"]. Shame! So I say; but who

is to blame? "There is no North," said Mr. Webster.
There is none. The South goes clear up to the Canada
line. No, gentlemen, there is no Boston to-day. There
was a Boston once. Now, there is a north suburb to the
city of Alexandria; that is what Boston is [laughter].
And you and I, fellow-subjects of the State of Virginia
[cries of "no," "no"]. I will take it back when you
show me the fact is not so. Men and brothers (brothers,
at any rate), I am an old man; I have heard hurrahs and
cheers for liberty many times; I have not seen a great
many *deeds* done for liberty. I ask you, are we to have
deeds as well as words? [" yes," "yes," and loud cheers.]

Now, brethren, — you are brothers at any rate, whether
citizens of Massachusetts or subjects of Virginia,— (I am
a minister), and, fellow-citizens of Boston, there are two
great laws in this country; one of them is the LAW OF
SLAVERY; that law is declared to be a "finality." Once
the Constitution was formed "to establish justice, promote
tranquility, and secure the blessings of liberty to ourselves
and our posterity." *Now*, the Constitution is *not* to secure
liberty; it is to *extend slavery* into Nebraska; and, when
slavery is established there, in order to show what it is,
there comes a sheriff from Alexandria to kidnap a man in
the city of Boston, and he gets a Judge of Probate, in the
county of Suffolk, to issue a writ, and a Boston man to
execute that writ! [cries of " shame," "shame."]

Slavery tramples on the Constitution; it treads down
State rights. Where are the rights of Massachusetts?
A Fugitive Slave Law Commissioner has got them all in
his pocket. Where is the trial by jury? Watson Freeman has it under his Marshal's staff. Where is the great
right of personal replevin, which our fathers wrested, several hundred years ago, from the tyrants who once lorded

it over Great Britain? Judge Sprague trod it under his feet! Where is the sacred right of *habeas corpus*? Deputy Marshal Riley can crush it in his hands, and Boston does not say anything against it. Where are the laws of Massachusetts forbidding state edifices to be used as prisons for the incarceration of fugitives? They, too, are trampled under foot. " Slavery is a finality."

These men came from Virginia to kidnap a man here. Once, this was Boston; now, it is a northern suburb of Alexandria. At first, when they carried a fugitive slave from Boston, they thought it was a difficult thing to do it. They had to get a Mayor to help them; they had to put chains round the Court House; they had to call out the " Sims' Brigade; " it took nine days to do it. Now, they are so confident that we are subjects of Virginia that they do not even put chains round the Court House; the police have nothing to do with it. I was told, to-day, that one of the officers of the city said to twenty-eight policemen, if any man in the employment of the city meddles in this business, he will be discharged from service without a hearing, [great applause]. Well, gentlemen, how do you think they received that declaration? They shouted, and hurrahed, and gave three cheers, [renewed applause.] My friend here would not have the honor of presiding over you to-night, if application had been made a little sooner to the Mayor. Another gentleman told me that, when he was asked to preside at this meeting, he said that he regretted that all his time to-night was previously engaged. If he had known it earlier, he said, he might have been able to make arrangements to preside. When the man was arrested, he told the Marshal he regretted it, and that his sympathies were wholly with the slave, [loud applause]. Fellow-citizens, remember that word. Hold

your Mayor to it, and let it be seen that he has got a
background, and a foreground, which will authorize him to
repeat that word in public, and act it out in Faneuil Hall.
I say, so confident are the slave agents now that they can
carry off their slave, in the day-time, that they do not put
chains round the Court House; they have got no soldiers
billeted in Faneuil Hall, as in 1851. They think they
can carry this man off to-morrow morning in a cab, [voices
— " they can't do it " — " let 's see them try"].

I say, there are two great laws in this country. One is
the slave law : that is the law of the President of the
United States; it is Senator Douglas's law; it is the law
of the Supreme Court of the United States; it is the law
of the Commissioner; it is the law of every Marshal, and
of every meanest ruffian whom the Marshal hires to execute his behests. There is another law, which my friend,
Mr. Phillips, has described in language such as I cannot
equal, and therefore shall not try ; I only state it in its
plainest terms. It is the law of the people, when they are
sure they are right and determined to go ahead, [cheers].

Now, gentlemen, there was a Boston once, and you and
I had fathers — brave fathers; and mothers who stirred
up those fathers to manly deeds. Well, gentlemen, once
it came to pass that the British Parliament enacted a
" law " — *they* called it a law — issuing stamps here. What
did your fathers do on that occasion? They said, in the
language of Algernon Sydney, quoted in your resolutions,
" That which is not just is not law, and that which is not
law ought not to be obeyed," [cheers]. They did not obey
the stamp act. They did not call it a *law*, and the man
that did call it a law here, eighty years ago, would have
had a very warm coat of tar and feathers on him. They
called it an " act," and they took the Commissioner who

25*

was here to execute it, took him solemnly, manfully, — *they didn't harm a hair of his head;* they were non-resistants of a very potent sort [laughter], — and made him take a solemn oath that he would not issue a single stamp. He was brother-in-law of the Governor of the State, the servant of a royal master, exceedingly respectable, of great wealth, and once very popular; but they took him, and made him swear not to execute his commission; and he kept his oath, and the stamp act went to its own place, and you know what that was, [cheers]. That was an instance of the people going behind a wicked law to enact absolute justice into their justice, and making it common law. You know what they did with the tea.

Well, gentlemen, in the South there is a public opinion (it is a very wicked public opinion), which is stronger than law. When a colored seaman goes to Charleston from Boston he is clapped instantly into jail, and kept there until the vessel is ready to sail, and the Boston merchant or master must pay the bill, and the Boston black man must feel the smart. That is a wicked example, set by the State of South Carolina. When Mr. Hoar, one of our most honored and respected fellow-citizens, was sent to Charleston, to test the legality of this iniquitous law, the citizens of Charleston ordered him off the premises, and he was glad to escape, to save himself from further insult. There was no violence, no guns fired. This is an instance of the *strength of public opinion* — of a most unjust and iniquitous public opinion.

Well, gentlemen, I say there is one law — slave law; it is everywhere. There is another law, which also is a finality; and that law, it is in your hands and your arms, and you can put that in execution just when you see fit. Gentlemen, I am a clergyman and a man of peace; I love peace. But there is a means, and there is an end; liberty is the end, and sometimes peace is not the means towards it [applause]. Now I want to ask you what you are going to do [a voice — "shoot, shoot"]. There are ways of managing this matter, without shooting anybody. Be sure that these men who have kidnapped a man in Boston are cowards, every mother's son of them; and, if we stand up there resolutely, and declare that this man shall not go out of the city of Boston, *without shooting a gun* — [cries of "that's it," and great applause], — then he won't go back. Now, I am going to propose that when you adjourn, it be to meet in *Court Square to-morrow morning at 9 o'clock.* As many as are in favor of that motion will raise their hands, [a large number of hands were raised, but many voices cried out, "Let's go to-night," "let's pay a visit to the slave-catchers at the Revere House," etc., etc.] Do you propose to go to the Revere House to-night? then show your hands, [some hands were held up]. It is not a vote. We shall meet in *Court Square at 9 o'clock to-morrow morning.*

DATE DUE